CRASH COURSE

H̲ Recording

Printed and bound in the UK by MPG Books Ltd, Bodmin, Cornwall

Published in the UK by SMT, an imprint of Sanctuary Publishing Limited, Sanctuary House, 45-53 Sinclair Road, London W14 0NS, United Kingdom

www.sanctuarypublishing.com

ISBN: 1-84492-017-8

Home Recording

Paul White

smt

This book is dedicated to my wife, Christine, and my daughter, Emma

CONTENTS

WEEK 4
MIXERS

WEEK 5
EFFECTS AND PROCESSORS

WEEK 6
MONITORING———————————————————————————————— 119

WEEK 7
MULTITRACK RECORDING———————————————————————— 129

INTRODUCTION

Welcome to *Crash Course Home Recording*, which is written for the complete beginner and explores the key basic principles that will enable you to make high-quality recordings of your own with very little equipment. When the publishers first asked me to undertake this project, I felt they'd asked for the impossible, as the whole field of recording is immense and covers tape machines, hard-disk recorders, digital and analogue technology, microphones, mixing, signal processing and a whole host of other disciplines. However, after giving the project some thought, I realised that it wasn't the mechanics of recording that caused most people problems; after all, at its most basic, making a good recording is simply a matter of selecting the right microphone and putting it in the right place within a suitable acoustic space in order to capture a musical performance as accurately as possible. Once you can do this, understanding multitrack recording and mixing isn't such a big deal.

Most of this book deals with these essential basic principles, presented in as non-technical a way as possible. This information will help you to progress quickly in whatever type of recording interests you, but the concepts of mixers, mixing, multitrack recording and signal processing are also introduced so that you'll know where to go next. Because much of the book covers basic principles, you don't need any expensive equipment to work through the techniques discussed here, though you may need to spend a little money on a decent-quality microphone or two, a small mixer and some kind of stereo recorder. You'll always need microphones, no matter what type of recording you move into, so your purchases should never become obsolete.

Home Recording

Simply read as much as you feel comfortable with in one sitting and, where possible, try out the techniques discussed using your own recording equipment, even if it's just a couple of mics and a MiniDisc recorder. I've included a few questions at the end of each section so that you can confirm you've understood everything covered over the course of each week. Practical experience is essential if you are to become proficient at recording – but then, you wouldn't be reading this if you weren't keen to try things out for yourself, would you?

WEEK 1

THE ESSENCE OF RECORDING

I've tried to keep this book as non-technical as possible, but as with any technology-based subject there are a few basic principles that you need to be aware of if what follows is to make sense. This first week looks at those principles on a 'need to know' basis, and I've tried to avoid burdening you with information you don't need to know. Other snippets will be introduced as needed, but I promise that there will be nothing too heavy – most of this book is about getting good, practical results with minimum complexity. If you really can't face reading the background info first, you can always refer back to it if you come across a concept or term later on in the book that you don't understand.

SOUNDS AND SIGNALS

As we're all taught at school, sound is the result of the atmosphere 'vibrating' in response to a vibrating object, such as a bell, a guitar string or a set of human vocal cords. These atmospheric vibrations take the form of rapid changes of air pressure, and if you were able to see these vibrations, you'd see that they come in short cycles where the air is first compressed and then rarefied before the cycle starts again. Our eardrums detect these pressure changes and convert them into nerve impulses that our brains perceive as sound (provided that the vibrations are within the frequency range of human hearing). The textbooks tell us that this is approximately 20Hz–20kHz, but in reality only people with very good hearing can hear sounds pitched as high as 20kHz.

Home Recording

The term *Hertz* (Hz) replaced the far more logical term *cycles*, which in the case of sound simply describes how many times each second the sound source (and, consequently, the air) repeats its vibration pattern. Figure 1.1 shows how a sound wave travels by compressing and rarefying the air.

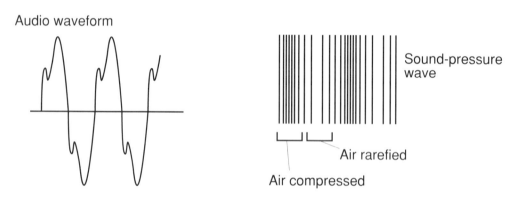

Figure 1.1: Sound waves travel by alternately compressing and rarefying the air

We humans, and most animals, have two ears – and not just for the reason that it's good to have a spare! Sound travels at approximately 300 metres per second, which means that, if a sound originates from one side of us, it arrives at one ear very slightly before it arrives at the other. Our brains can perceive this delay and use it (amongst other sonic clues) to estimate the direction from which the sound is coming. The other main sonic clue is the level or volume of the sound reaching the two ears, because if a sound comes from one side, the masking effect of the head will cause an acoustic shadow that makes the sound entering the furthest ear less loud than that picked up by the ear facing the sound source. If, on the other hand, a sound originates from directly in front of us, it will reach both ears at the same time

and will be equal in level at both ears. The way in which we work out whether a sound is directly in front or behind us is in part linked to the shape of our outer ears and how they affect the tonality of sound approaching from different directions, but for the purpose of this introduction the most important thing to note is that the relative levels and time difference between the sounds arriving at our two ears are mainly responsible for our being able to deduce the direction of their source.

STEREO

We call the ability to determine the direction of a sound source by using two ears *stereophonic hearing*, and since the 1950s audio engineers have been building stereo recording and playback systems that make it possible to trick the ears into believing that different sounds in a recording are coming from different directions, even though the two speakers are in fixed positions.

The basic principle of stereo is fairly simple. If you space two directional mics (those that 'hear' mainly in one direction) apart to approximate the distance between our ears and point them away from each other to some degree, you can record what they pick up in a way that keeps the two signals separate (this is what a stereo recorder does), then use these separate signals on playback to feed two spaced speakers or a pair of headphones to recreate something approximating the original experience, complete with those important directional sonic clues. How well this works depends on the characteristics of the mics and where they are placed, and as we shall see, we're not bound by the geometry of the human head when it comes to deciding how widely to space the mics. Figure 1.2 shows a stereo recording and playback chain.

Home Recording

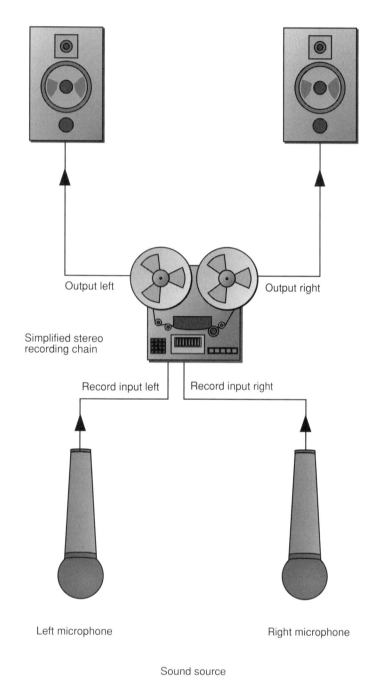

Output left

Output right

Simplified stereo recording chain

Record input left   Record input right

Left microphone   Right microphone

Sound source

Figure 1.2: Stereo recording and playback chain

EXERCISE

It's a useful exercise to close your eyes and listen to the sounds around you and then try to pick out the direction of the source. Try to notice how the quality or tonality of the sound changes as the source moves (or as you turn your head), and in particular try to hear the difference between a sound directly behind you and the same sound directly in front of you.

Also listen to some good stereo recordings over headphones and see if you can visualise the locations of the different instruments and voices. You can also do this with loudspeakers, but in this case it's important that you're sitting in the correct position relative to the speakers to hear the best stereo effect. Ideally this will be around two metres in front of the speakers and sitting on an imaginary line passing directly between the speakers so that your listening setup is perfectly symmetrical. Figure 1.3 shows the correct stereo monitoring/listening position over loudspeakers.

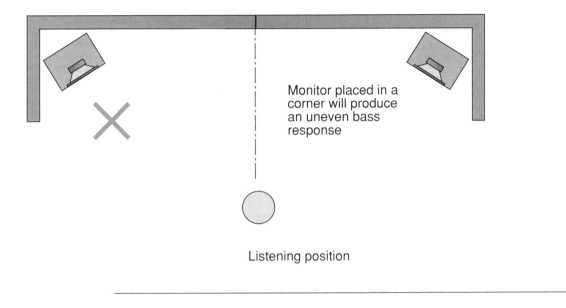

Monitor placed in a corner will produce an uneven bass response

Listening position

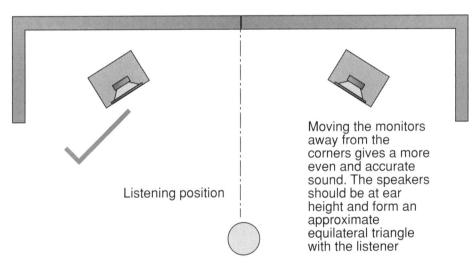

Moving the monitors away from the corners gives a more even and accurate sound. The speakers should be at ear height and form an approximate equilateral triangle with the listener

Listening position

Figure 1.3: Correct stereo monitoring/listening position using loudspeakers

PANNING

Although our ears use a number of different mechanisms to determine the direction of a sound source, varying the relative levels of the signals entering the left and right ears is often enough to fool the brain into thinking that the sound is

coming more from the left or right. This principle is used extensively in pop recording, where a mono recording made with a single microphone may be shifted left or right using a pan (short for *panorama*) control to change the balance of the signal feeding the left and right speakers or headphones. Feeding equal amounts of the audio signal to the left and right speakers makes it seem as if the sound is coming from exactly halfway between the speakers. Panning can only recreate the effect of left/right positioning and cannot normally make the sound source appear to be outside the area bounded by the two loudspeakers.

ABOUT MICS AND PREAMPS

The air vibrations that carry sound are usually very small and consequently carry very little energy. The purpose of a microphone is to convert the pressure variation in the air to voltage variations at the microphone's output, and this electrical output is known as an *audio signal*. Because the amount of sound energy intercepted by the microphone is small, the resulting audio signal will also be small, so it's necessary to amplify this signal electronically in order to make it big enough to be useful. (An amplifier is simply an electronic device that takes a signal and makes it larger without changing it in any other way.)

In audio work, we tend to reserve the term *amplifier* for a device that boosts signals to the level at which they can drive loudspeakers, so when it comes to amplifying microphone signals to make them large enough to record onto something like a tape machine or MiniDisc recorder, we tend to use the term *preamplifier*. Some recorders have built-in microphone preamplifiers whose job is to boost the mic signal up to

what's known as *line level*, which is typically a few volts. Most audio equipment is designed to work at line level, so if your recorder doesn't have microphone preamplifiers built into it, you'll need to connect a suitable preamplifier between the microphone and the recorder. Figure 1.4 shows a pair of microphones (for stereo recording) connected to a recorder via a stereo (dual-channel) preamplifier.

Figure 1.4: Pair of microphones (for stereo recording) connected to a recorder via a stereo (dual-channel) preamplifier

Stereo power amplifier

Output left   Output right

Simplified stereo recording chain

Recorder line input left   Recorder line input right

Two-channel mic preamp

For stereo recording, mics may be spaced omnis, spaced cardioids or coincident cardioids

Coincident cardioids

Spaced microphone pair

Left microphone   Right microphone

Sound source

Home Recording

If the term capacitor microphones means nothing to you, don't worry as it will be explained in Week 2, 'Microphones And Their Uses'. Suffice it to say that capacitor mics are generally the best choice for serious audio recording as they produce the most accurate sound, especially at the important higher frequencies, and they also help to minimise background hiss when recording quiet sound sources. Where does hiss come from? It's all to do with physics plus something called *gain structure*.

GAIN STRUCTURE

The human ear can hear sounds ranging in level from the dropping of a pin to the firing of a cannon, and even the very best recording equipment fails to match its dynamic range. In music, we never need to go to these extremes, but even so a line-level musical signal may fluctuate from just a few microvolts (millionths of a volt) in strength, in the very quiet passages, up to perhaps around 20V or so at the loudest peaks.

All pieces of audio electronic equipment, whether analogue or digital (and I'll go into what these terms signify later), produce a more or less constant level of background hiss, the minimum level of which is determined by the laws of physics. You can never get rid of noise altogether unless you cool everything to Absolute Zero, in which case you'd probably be more concerned about finding a coat and a nice thick pair of socks than listening for hiss!

In well-designed equipment, this hiss or noise is so low in level as to be inaudible under normal circumstances because the wanted audio signal is very much bigger than the noise and so masks it in much the same way that a low-flying jet would mask the rustle of leaves on next door's tree. However, if you inadvertently pass an audio signal that is much lower in level than it's supposed to be through a piece of equipment, it may no longer be significantly louder than the noise, so when you turn up the overall level so that you can hear the audio normally, the hiss will also be turned up and may become audible.

This seems to imply that all we have to do is record everything at as high a level as possible, and this is true to some extent, but there's another danger waiting for us at the other end of the scale. All equipment has a maximum signal level at which it can work, and if you try to exceed that level, the shape of the audio signal will no longer be an accurate representation of the input, and you'll hear this as unpleasant-sounding audio distortion. What all this amounts to is that, for every piece of electronic equipment in the signal path, you need to adjust the gain controls so that each device is passing as high a level of signal as possible, as

Home Recording

long as the signal never gets so high that it exceeds the maximum level and becomes distorted. In the practical world, this is done with gain controls (which determine the degree to which amplifiers amplify) and meters (which show the audio signal level relative to the permitted maximum level).

In the case of our simple system using two mics, a two-channel preamp and a stereo recorder, this would mean adjusting the preamp gain control to show a healthy output level on the meters and also adjusting the input-level control on the recorder to make sure that the signal is as high as permissible. In music recording, these adjustments are normally made when the performer is running through the piece, including those sections that are likely to be loudest.

TOP TIP

Remember that if you record at too low a level, your recording will be noisier (ie more hissy) than it should be, whereas if you record at too high a level, the sound will become distorted, so always check the meters on your recorder prior to recording and then make a test recording to ensure that the levels don't change too much. It's always wise to leave a little safety margin on the meters – where signal levels are expressed in dB (decibels) – as musicians often play slightly louder once they get warmed up! Also keep an eye on the meters during recording, just in case the musician suddenly gets louder than he or she did in the initial run-through.

Note: On analogue tape recorders, the meters can go a little way into the red on the loudest parts of your music, as the onset of distortion above this point is gradual, and anyway a little distortion is not normally audible. However, digital recording systems, such as MiniDisc, have no safety margin, so you have to ensure that your signals are as high as possible without ever causing the peak or clip indicators to light. When it comes to avoiding the risk of exceeding the maximum input level on a digital recorder, the nominal safe operating level is usually around 12dB or so below the oVU 'clipping' point, as this leaves a realistic safety margin to guard against unexpectedly loud musical phrases while still leaving the signal high enough in level to avoid noise problems.

To recap, the whole point of paying attention to gain structure is to ensure that every piece of audio equipment in your system is running at or close to its optimum signal level. This means not only optimising your recording levels but also the levels of any signals fed into your mixer, if you have one. Week 4 is devoted entirely to mixers, but here it's enough to know that conceptually they are devices comprising multiple preamplifiers, along with the means of combining or mixing the signals coming from the various preamplifier outputs into a single (mono) or two-channel (stereo) signal. The relative levels of all the contributing signals can also be adjusted, and there may be other features, such as EQ (a fancy name for tone controls) and the ability to route signals through other signal processors or effects boxes, such as electronic reverb units. (If you do have any signal-processing devices plugged into your mixer, you also have to make sure they're receiving healthy signal levels.)

Home Recording

Although optimising gain structure may sound unnecessarily technical in a process that's supposed to be about capturing art, it's really just a matter of being methodical and making sure your meter readings are sensible at every stage along the signal path before you start recording. The difference this can make to the quality of the end result can be huge.

IMPEDANCE

Most people will have come across the electrical term *resistance*, which can be thought of as being analogous to somebody standing on a water pipe when you're trying to pump water through it. The harder they stand on the pipe, the more resistance there is and the harder you have to pump the water to maintain the flow. In electrical terms, resistance is what restricts the flow of electric current.

Whereas resistance relates to constant levels of current (direct current, or DC), impedance can be thought of as being a circuit's resistance to an alternating current, such as an audio signal. In many audio circuits, the impedance will vary in response to the frequency of the signal passing through it. Fortunately, you don't need know much about impedance, other than the fact that it exists and that it's important for the pieces equipment in your audio chain to match each other, impedance-wise.

Most of the recording equipment used in project studios will connect together without any impedance concerns, but you should be aware that the vast majority of serious studio microphones are termed 'low impedance' and so will work only when connected to preamps designed for use with low-impedance microphones.

Fortunately, studio equipment is invariably designed to work with low-impedance mics, although some consumer equipment is designed to work with high-impedance models and so won't work properly with studio microphones.

TOP TIP

If a microphone has a three-pin XLR connector rather than a fixed cable, it's almost certainly low impedance and probably also balanced. (I'll explain what *balanced* means in Week 2, 'Microphones And Their Uses'.) Similarly, if a mic preamp has a three-pin XLR input, it will invariably be designed to work with low-impedance microphones. Mics fitted with mono jack plugs may be high-impedance models, in which case they will work only with equipment that has a high-impedance microphone input – for example, some domestic recorders and less sophisticated PA mixer/amplifiers.

WARNING: In most cases, studio equipment will allow you to split a line-level source signal to feed two or more destinations. Note, however, that you can't mix audio signals by joining two outputs together as the signal is likely to be seriously distorted, and you also run the risk of damaging your equipment.

LINE LEVELS

Just to complicate matters, there are two 'standard' line levels in common use in audio circles: the −10dBV standard (for semi-pro and domestic recording

Home Recording

equipment, such as hi-fis) and the +4dBu standard (for pro studio gear). Don't worry if these terms don't mean much to you; various broadcasting institutions use different levels still, but most are close enough that you can use one with the other, provided that you set your gain controls correctly.

DECIBELS

The decibel (dB) is a throwback to the pioneering days of telephones – indeed, its name comes from the device's creator, Alexander Graham Bell – but at least it's a standard, of sorts. It's often used as a convenient way of expressing the ratio between two signal levels. The decibel scale is logarithmic, just like the human ear, so decibels on a VU meter correspond pretty closely to our perceived impression of loudness. The maximum signal level on a VU meter is usually shown as 0dB with lower levels marked as so many decibels below this (shown as decibels with a minus sign) on the meter scale. Figure 1.5 shows both moving-coil (ie the type with a pointer) and bar-graph VU meters. Digital equipment almost always uses bar-graph meters as they are able to respond faster to changes in level, and it's important to know if a signal is likely to exceed the maximum level, even if only for a very brief period.

Because decibels are logarithmic, most calculations (not that you normally have to do any – don't panic!) involve addition or subtraction rather than multiplication or division, which makes life easy for a change. For example, doubling a signal voltage corresponds to a 6dB increase, so making the voltage four times as big would equate to a 12dB increase. There are formulae for calculating decibel ratios, but, being practical, most of the time you're just concerned with having enough of them

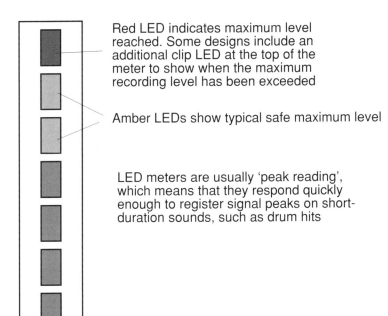

Red LED indicates maximum level reached. Some designs include an additional clip LED at the top of the meter to show when the maximum recording level has been exceeded

Amber LEDs show typical safe maximum level

LED meters are usually 'peak reading', which means that they respond quickly enough to register signal peaks on short-duration sounds, such as drum hits

Peak-reading bar-graph meter

Figure 1.5a: Bar-graph VU meter

Start of red area denotes maximum recording level, although with analogue machines – on which some overload is acceptable – it is common to have the meter peaking into the red area

Moving-coil VU meter

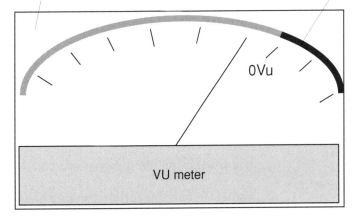

VU meter

Figure 1.5b: Moving-coil VU meter

Because of their mechanical intertia, moving-coil meters are unable to register accurate short-duration signal-peak levels and instead tend to follow the average signal level. They are well suited for use with analogue processors and recorders, on which brief periods of signal overload can be tolerated, but are less useful in digital systems, where maximum really means maximum!

showing on your level meters without the red 'Oops, too much' light coming on.
Musical instruments, such as electronic pianos, drum machines and synths, have
line-level outputs, as do mic preamps and guitar recording preamps. Of course,
some may be at the lower consumer –10dBV level or lower, although these can still
be connected directly to a preamp's or mixer's line-level input, as long as you adjust
the preamp gain control accordingly.

Electric guitars, on the other hand, produce relatively small outputs, and because
of the way in which the pickups are designed, they need to be used with a special
high-impedance preamplifier where the input impedance is around one mega-
ohm (1 million ohms). For this reason, when not recording by miking the guitar
amplifier, it is invariably better to use a purpose-built guitar preamplifier or active
DI box (a special type of preamp with a high input impedance) rather than
plugging the guitar directly into a preamp's or mixer's line-level input.

DIGITAL AUDIO

Analogue electronics is based on a system whereby changes in input signal cause
a change in output signal – almost the electronic equivalent of a system of pulleys
and levers. The input signal is a constantly changing voltage and so is the output
signal. To use the earlier analogy of squashing a hosepipe to restrict the flow of
water, you could say that the varying pressure of the foot is the input signal and
the corresponding varying flow of water is the output signal. Analogue is simple
and it sounds good, but the output is never quite a perfect copy of the input, so
the more analogue stages a signal passes through, the more it is changed or

distorted and the more noise is added. Mic preamps are analogue devices, as are most conventional power amps, guitar amps and basic mixers, but as tape recorders have now been largely replaced by digital recorders, effects processors tend to be digital and many of the more sophisticated mixers are also digital. But what exactly is 'digital'?

DIGITAL BASICS

Whereas analogue systems use circuitry to make the output constantly follow changes in the input, digital systems take analogue signals (such as the outputs from microphones) and convert them into what is effectively a series of binary numbers (ones and zeros) prior to processing or recording. These digital converters (or analogue-to-digital converters, to give them their correct name) measure the incoming voltage at very closely spaced, regular intervals. So, instead of the output being a varying voltage, as it is with analogue, it's now a string of binary numbers, each representing the level of the input signal at the time it was measured or sampled. If you have enough instantaneous measurements per second, the original sound can be accurately recreated up to the highest frequency limit of human hearing, although this requires tens of thousands of samples per second.

At the output of the digital system, where an analogue signal is again needed to drive loudspeakers via a power amplifier, a digital-to-analogue converter reverses the process and converts the numbers back to their original voltages, thus reconstructing the original signal. While information is in the digital domain, it can be copied exactly simply by duplicating the digital data (numbers), so it is

possible to transfer (clone) digital data without degradation – something that's quite impossible with analogue recordings.

SAMPLING THEORY

Figure 1.6 shows what happens when a signal is sampled. Each sample is a discrete measurement taken at one instant in time, and the more often these are taken, the more accurately the curves of the original analogue signal are followed. It turns out that you must sample at a minimum of twice the frequency of the highest frequency you're likely to encounter if the output is to be reconstructed accurately. If the

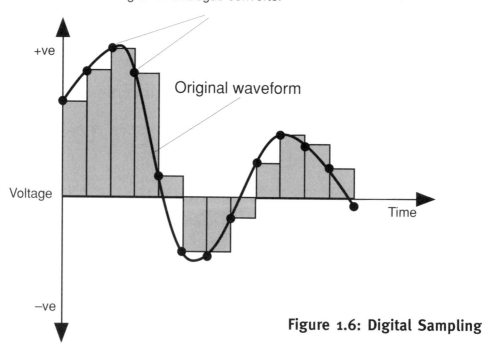

The signal voltage is sampled at regular intervals and the instantaneous values measured as binary numbers. The original signal can be reconstructed from this digital data in a digital-to-analogue converter

Original waveform

Figure 1.6: Digital Sampling

sampling frequency is less than twice the highest frequency, additional frequencies will be introduced that were never present in the original signal, and they tend to sound pretty unmusical. These additional frequencies are based on the sum and difference between the sampling frequency and the audio frequency, and so, harmonically speaking, are completely unrelated to the original signal.

This effect is known as *aliasing*, and in order to prevent it the converter must first filter out any frequencies in the original signal that are above half the sampling frequency. (For those interested in such things, this is explained by the Nyquist theory.) Because no filter is perfect, the sampling rate must be made a little higher than twice the maximum audio frequency, and in the case of audio CDs, which have an upper audio-frequency limit of 20kHz, the sampling rate is 44.1kHz. And yes, 44.1kHz is an odd kind of number to choose – after all, why not 45kHz or 50kHz? – but that's engineers for you.

Having established that we need to take many samples, we also have to measure those samples accurately or the sound will be noisy and/or distorted. As you might imagine, the more digital bits are used to represent each sample, the more accurate the measurement. CDs use 16-bit sampling, although most digital multitrack recorders and signal processors now use 24-bit conversion.

Digital numbers go in whole-number (integer) steps – there are no halves or thirds of a bit. Eight bits will give you only two-to-the-power-of-eight steps, which works out at 256. This means that your loudest signal could have 256 steps, while

quieter ones will have considerably fewer. This gives a rather poor level of resolution and causes what's known as *quantisation distortion*, a side-effect that sounds like noise, except it disappears in the absence of a signal. Using more bits gives a vast improvement in resolution and, in a conventional sampling system, equates to 6dB of dynamic range per bit. An eight-bit system can give you a dynamic range of only 48dB at best – about as noisy as a cheap cassette recorder. Sixteen bits gives a maximum range of 96dB (the standard audio-CD format), while 24-bit systems can give dynamic ranges in excess of 120dB. Simplistically, dynamic range is the difference between the loudest signal a system can handle and the quietest signal. From a music-recording perspective, the more dynamic range the better, because it means less background noise and less distortion.

SAMPLE RATES

If CDs work at a sampling rate of 44.1kHz, why do we see equipment with 48kHz and even 96kHz sample rates? For historic reasons, CDs use the 44.1kHz sample rate, but broadcasters (and video DVD soundtracks) use a 48kHz sample rate. Some recorders and soundcards can be switched between two or more sample rates.

 It is crucial that everything in a digital system (where the interconnections between the pieces of equipment are digital rather than analogue) runs at the same sample rate. Recent system have been introduced that run at double the current standard sampling rates, so now we can add 88.2kHz and 96kHz to the list. In theory, these produce a slightly better sound quality, but in practice few people can detect a difference.

 Not only must all the digital elements of a system run at the same sample rate but their clocks must also run in perfect sync, otherwise errors find their way into the audio signal, manifesting themselves as pops and clicks. This synchronisation is normally achieved by designating the device containing the analogue-to-digital converters as the master clock for the system and setting the other devices later in the chain to External Sync mode. This way, the other devices pick up the clock signal from the master unit, and it is then passed along the interconnecting cable along with the audio data.

DIGITAL CONNECTIONS

Stereo digital audio is normally transferred between devices either by the S/PDIF connection system (developed by Sony and Philips) or by the balanced AES/EBU system. The data structure between the two formats is identical, the only difference being that S/PDIF carries different *data flags* – most importantly, those to do with copy protection, which are included in some commercial material to prevent unlicensed copying. S/PDIF (generally pronounced 'spidiff') comes in two varieties, optical (Toslink format) or co-axial (which uses RCA phono connectors), although third-party boxes are available that can convert between the two. AES/EBU uses balanced XLRs, just like microphones, but although mic cable will work over modest distances, it's best to buy purpose-made digital cables for both S/PDIF and AES/EBU connection as the cable needs to have a specific impedance in order to prevent errors from creeping in.

Home Recording

WEEK 1 TEST

OK, so you've reached the end of Week 1. Now here are a few questions to make sure you've absorbed the information covered in the previous section.

1 Which control would you use to make a mono signal appear to be positioned at one side or the other in a stereo recording?

2 Why is it important to avoid exceeding the input limit with digital equipment?

3 If you wish to record an audio signal, the highest frequency of which is 20kHz, into a digital system, what must the minimum sampling rate be?

4 Which gives the greatest dynamic range, a 16-bit recording system or a 24-bit system?

WEEK 2

MICROPHONES AND THEIR USES

Before getting started with some practical recording, I first need to explain a little bit about microphones. Again, I've kept everything very simple and left out everything technical where possible. Essentially, the job of a microphone is to convert sound energy into electrical energy as faithfully as possible. There are many different types of microphone construction, but all utilise some form of lightweight diaphragm that moves in response to the rapid fluctuations in air pressure that we know as sound. The difficult part is in effectively converting the movement of this diaphragm into an electrical signal.

Although microphone technology isn't perfect, it's now possible to buy extremely good microphones for recording uses at a fraction of the price they cost a decade or two ago, not least due to the fact that many of these microphones are now being mass-produced for the home recording market in Far Eastern countries. As far as home recording is concerned, we are mainly concerned with two types of microphone: the dynamic and the capacitor.

DYNAMIC MICROPHONES

At the heart of the dynamic (or 'moving-coil') microphone is a circular diaphragm made from a thin plastic film, attached to which is a very fine coil of wire that moves freely in a cylindrical gap in a permanent magnet. The motion of the coil within the magnetic field produces an electrical current that follows the movement of the diaphragm. Figure 2.1 shows the construction of a typical moving-coil microphone.

Home Recording

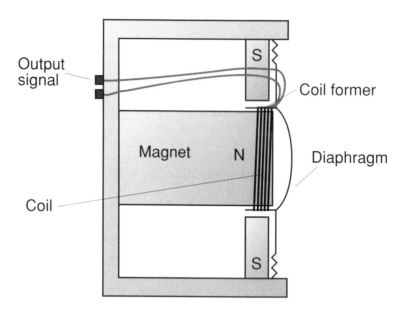

Figure 2.1: Structure of a dynamic microphone

Dynamic microphones have the advantage that they are relatively inexpensive and physically robust. They can also tolerate extremely high sound-pressure levels and require no power supply as there is no electronic circuitry within the microphone itself.

The main disadvantage of dynamic mics is that the mass of the coil attached to the diaphragm increases its inertia, so higher frequencies are not captured as well as lower frequencies. A typical dynamic microphone may work effectively up to around 16kHz but its performance falls off at higher frequencies. Furthermore, the electrical signal produced by a dynamic microphone is very small and so requires a lot of amplification to take it up to line level. At normal sound levels, this isn't a

serious issue, but quiet or distant sounds may need to be amplified so much that background noise becomes a problem.

Dynamic mics are often used for miking live vocals, drums (both live and recorded) and instrument amplifiers. In the studio, they tend to be used mainly for close-miking drums and for miking guitar amplifiers, although they can be useful for vocal recording, too, if you don't need the detailed high end provided by a capacitor microphone.

CAPACITOR MICROPHONES

A capacitor (or condenser, as it used to be called) comprises a pair of parallel metal plates separated by an insulator, such as air. These plates can store an electrical charge, and if the capacitance is then varied by altering the distance between the two plates, the voltage across the plates will also change. If one of these plates is a thin, conductive diaphragm that moves in response to changes in air pressure and the other is a fixed plate, the capacitor can be turned into a microphone by monitoring the voltage change at the capsule using a special preamplifier (built into the microphone).

A typical capacitor microphone capsule comprises a fixed metal plate separated by a small air gap from a very thin, flexible plastic diaphragm onto which has been deposited a thin metal coating to make it electrically conductive. This capsule needs a power source to generate the required electrical charge and the internal mic preamp also needs power. To accommodate this need, the so-called phantom

powering system was developed, which provides a 48V DC power source along a conventional balanced mic cable.

The part of the microphone that actually picks up the sound and turns it into an electrical signal is known as the capsule, which in the case of a capacitor mic comprises the diaphragm, the back plate and the necessary spacers and insulators that keep them apart. A dynamic mic capsule comprises the diaphragm, voice coil and magnetic assembly.

Compared with dynamic microphones, capacitor models have very light diaphragms and so can respond better to higher frequencies. Capacitor mics are also more sensitive, which simply means that, for a given sound level, they generate a larger output signal than a dynamic mic. This in turn means that electrical noise is less of a problem when working with quieter sound sources. Figure 2.2 shows the schematic of a capacitor mic.

While most dynamic mics have the capsule pointing towards the end of the mic, most large-capsule capacitor mics have it mounted sideways, so you sing into the side of the mic, not into the end. The manufacturer's logo usually indicates the live side of a cardioid mic.

Figure 2.2: Structure of a capacitor microphone

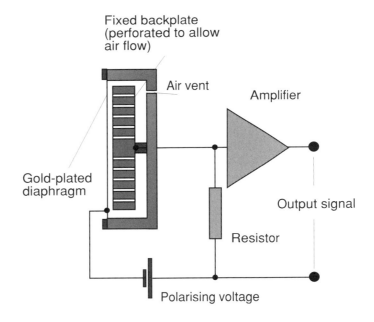

TOP TIP

Because of their ability to cover the entire audio spectrum, and because their high sensitivity allows them to be used with quieter or more distant sound sources, capacitor mics are usually the first choice for recording vocals and acoustic instruments and for use above a drum kit to capture the true sound of the cymbals. Some engineers also prefer them for recording guitar amplifiers.

ELECTRET MICROPHONES

No mention of the capacitor mic would be complete without mentioning the closely related electret mic. In an electret capsule, the electrical charge on the diaphragm is not provided by a power supply but instead is built in at manufacture by a process involving heat and strong magnetic fields. Cheaper

Home Recording

models have the charge-carrying elements built into the insulating material forming the diaphragm, but this results in a thicker diaphragm and the loss of many of the advantages of a true capacitor microphone.

By contrast, the so-called back-electret capsule can offer much better performance, and indeed can rival that of a true capacitor mic. This is because the electret material carrying the permanent electrical charge is instead fixed to the stationary back plate, allowing the moving diaphragm to be made of exactly the same ultra-lightweight material as that used in a true capacitor microphone.

Back-electret microphones still need power for their on-board preamps, but some models are available that can run on batteries as well as on phantom power.

VOICING

While it's possible to build a microphone with a very flat frequency response, it's sometimes advantageous to have one that adds its own character to the sound. For example, most live vocal mics have what is known as a *presence boost* at between 3kHz and 5kHz to add clarity to the sound and to help cut through the back line. A number of studio mics also have some degree of presence lift to create a brighter, more open sound, and as every designer has a different idea of what sounds best, all microphones sound slightly different from each other.

The other common modification to the frequency response is limiting the low-frequency sensitivity so that the mic isn't producing high-level, subsonic signals

due to floor vibrations or passing traffic. Some live vocal mics also have a greater

degree of *bass roll-off* to help counter the bass boost caused by the proximity effect

when singers work very close to the microphone. In some studio mics, these low-cut

filters can be activated via switches on the microphone body. Other switches (*pads*)

may be available to reduce the sensitivity of the microphone when subjected to very

loud sounds at close range.

Other tonal differences may be audible between mics with large-diameter capsules

and those with small-diameter capsules. As a rule, large-diaphragm mics are likely to

be more flattering while small diaphragm models tend to be more honest. There's also

often a subjective difference between mics with tube preamps and those with solid-

state preamps and between those that have transformer outputs and those that have

electronically balanced outputs. A lot of myth and lore has built up around

microphones, but excellent results can be achieved using well-chosen, budget

capacitor mics, most of which are large-diaphragm types. Note that large-capsule mics

tend to be 'side addrerss' while small-capsule 'stick' mics are invariably 'end address'.

DIRECTIONALITY

Most of the mics used in project studios are said to have unidirectional or cardioid

properties as they pick up sound mainly from in front of them and are less sensitive

at the sides and even less sensitive at the rear. However, not all microphones have

this directional characteristic, and the type that an engineer will choose to use will

depend on the requirements of the current recording job.

Home Recording

In fact there are three basic directional characteristics, known as *omnidirectional* (all directions), *cardioid* (meaning 'heart-shaped' – unidirectional) *and figure-of-eight* (which picks up from both front and rear but not from the sides). Some capacitor microphones incorporate two diaphragm assemblies, allowing them to be switched between the main directional pattern types, but as mentioned earlier, most project studio work relies on cardioid microphones as these are best at rejecting sound coming from directions other than in front of them. Fixed-pattern mics are invariably cheaper than those with switchable patterns.

CARDIOID MICROPHONES

Cardioid (unidirectional) microphones incorporate a specially designed sound path or labyrinth to delay the sounds reaching the rear of the diaphragm. Sounds arriving from the front of the microphone cause a difference in pressure between the front and rear of the diaphragm while sounds arriving from the rear and sides cause the difference in pressure to be less. It is this clever design feature that makes the cardioid mic (and its more directional cousin, the hypercardioid) most sensitive to sounds arriving from directly in front. The name *cardioid* comes from the graph of the mic's sensitivity, which looks roughly heart-shaped. Figure 2.3 shows the polar plot of a cardioid mic pattern.

Pressure-gradient microphones – both cardioids and the figure-of-eight type mentioned later – exhibit a characteristic known as the *proximity effect*, which causes low frequencies to be boosted quite significantly when the sound source

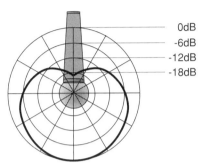

Cardioid:
Picks up sound mainly from the front. Least sensitive at the rear, making it a good choice for live performance

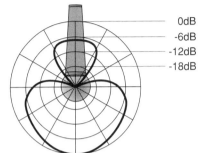

Hypercardioid:
Also called a supercardioid, this mic has a narrower pattern than the cardioid, but is more sensitive to sounds coming directly from behind

Figure 2.3: Polar plots of a cardioid and hypercardioid microphone

moves to within a few centimetres of the microphone. The physics behind this effect is quite complicated, but for practical purposes it's sufficient to know that it exists. Placing a pop shield in front of a vocal mic will prevent the singer from getting too close.

OMNIDIRECTIONAL MICROPHONES

An omnidirectional microphone comprises a diaphragm across the opening of a small metal chamber and measures air pressure much like a barometer (although there is a small hole in the chamber to prevent the diaphragm from moving in response to the weather!). Because pressure changes occur regardless of the direction of the sound source, the mic should be equally sensitive in all

directions. However, all microphones partly obstruct the soundfield, so the response of an omnidirectional mic is often less than perfect, especially with physically large models. This imperfection usually results in the mic's sensitivity to high frequencies being slightly less at the sides and rear than at the front.

Omnidirectional microphones do not exhibit the proximity effect inherent in cardioid and figure-of-eight designs. Although omnis pick up sound from all directions, and are thus more vulnerable to picking up sound leakage from behind the mic, they tend to have a more open, neutral sound than omnis, which has led to them being used extensively in the recording of classical music and acoustic performances in rooms with good acoustics. Figure 2.4 below shows an omnidirectional microphone pattern.

Figure 2.4: Polar plot of an omnidirectional microphone

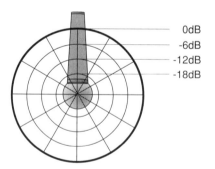

Omnidirectional: Picks up sound equally from all directions. Good for picking up multiple sound sources at the same time or for recording a sound along with the room ambience

FIGURE-OF-EIGHT MICROPHONES

The figure-of-eight-pattern microphone uses a diaphragm that's open to the air on both sides, so it's equally sensitive at the front and at the back. However, it picks up virtually nothing from the side, as sound arriving from the side will reach both sides of the diaphragm at exactly the same time. This means that the air pressure on both sides of the diaphragm will always be equal when sounds arrive from the side. No pressure difference means no movement of the diaphragm, hence no output signal. The name comes from the fact that the pickup pattern of the mic looks exactly like a figure eight, as shown in Figure 2.5.

Because this type of microphone's operating principle is based on the difference in pressure between the front and the rear, it's known as a *pressure-gradient*

Figure 2.5: Polar plot of a figure-of-eight microphone

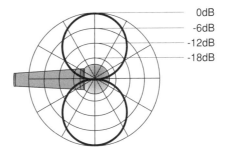

Figure of eight:
Picks up sound from both the front and rear of the capsule, but not from the sides. Used in specialist recording applications but may also be useful in situations where sounds coming from the side need to be rejected

microphone and exhibits a proximity effect – just like the cardioid mic – which results in an increase in the mic's responsiveness to low-frequency sounds when used very close to (ie within a few centimetres of) the source. Figure-of-eight mics tend to be used in fairly specialist or advanced applications, so it's not really appropriate to discuss them further in this book.

WHY ALL THESE PATTERNS?

Knowing these different directional patterns will allow you to choose the best mic for a specific situation. The cardioid should be your first choice where unwanted 'off-axis' sound – such as room reverberation or 'spill' from other instruments – needs to be minimised, and in home studios where space is limited and acoustic treatment often basic or non-existent, cardioids often provide the best solution.

Omnidirectional microphones sound more natural than cardioids and reproduce off-axis sounds reasonably faithfully. They exhibit no proximity effect, but as they pick up sound from all directions, they are best used in situations where spill from other directions is not a problem and where the room acoustics are sympathetic to the instrument or voice being recorded.

Figure-of-eight mics can be useful in situations where the side of the mic can be pointed in the direction of unwanted sound sources, as there's a very high level of rejection in this direction.

BALANCING

I've already mentioned balancing a couple of times, so I guess I can't get away without explaining it any longer! A conventional signal cable, such as a guitar lead or unbalanced mic cable, comprises a single, insulated centre core surrounded by a screen woven from fine wire and protected by an insulating sleeve. Such screened cable offers some protection against interference, and a good way of visualising the way it works is as interference being intercepted by the outer screen and then drained away to the electrical ground, which is where the screen is connected. This is slightly simplistic, but it's a good way to think about it.

In practice, because the screen is also one of the audio signal conductors, some proportion of the interfering signal still ends up added to the wanted signal from the microphone, and the longer the cable, the more likely it is that interference will be a problem.

Professional audio systems and all low-impedance microphones rely on the so-called *balanced system*, which uses two central cable cores, again surrounded by a protective screen. Unlike the unbalanced signal, however, the screen doesn't form part of the signal path – it's there purely to intercept interference and to tie the grounds of various pieces of equipment together.

In the case of microphones, both the microphone and the preamplifier to which it is connected must be designed for balanced operation in order for this system to work. Figure 2.6 shows how a balanced system is wired. The really clever part of

Home Recording

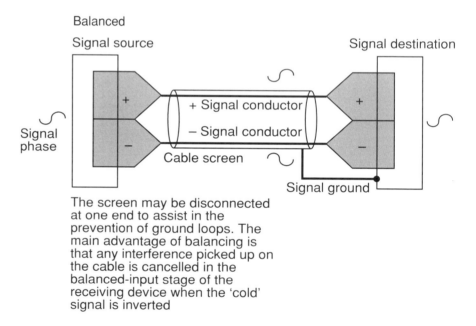

Unbalanced

Signal source

Signal destination

Signal phase

Signal conductor

Cable screen

Signal ground

Signal ground

Balanced

Signal source

Signal destination

Signal phase

+ Signal conductor

− Signal conductor

Cable screen

Signal ground

The screen may be disconnected at one end to assist in the prevention of ground loops. The main advantage of balancing is that any interference picked up on the cable is cancelled in the balanced-input stage of the receiving device when the 'cold' signal is inverted

Figure 2.6: Balanced cable system

balancing is that inside the microphone (or other audio device where line-level signals are involved) the output signal is split into two opposite phases, usually by means of a transformer or an electronic output balancing circuit. By 'phases' I mean that one output is inverted with respect to the other – when the voltage increases on one cable, it decreases by the same amount on the other. These two

phases are known as *positive and negative* or *hot and cold* and are fed down the two centre cores of the mic cable. The screen is connected to ground at one or both ends of the cable.

At the mixer or preamp end of the system, a balanced input stage adds another stage of phase inversion, which has the effect of putting the signal back the way it was before it was sent into the balanced system. When these two audio signals – which are now back in phase – are combined, the signal level is doubled, but any interference that was picked up by the cable largely cancels itself out.

PHANTOM POWER

Capacitor and electret microphones and active DI boxes require power to operate, and the most common way of providing this in the studio is via *phantom power*, so called because it requires no special cables and so is 'invisible'. The standard phantom power-supply voltage requirement for microphones is 48V, and this is provided by most mixers and preamps. A preamp that provides phantom power supplies the necessary DC power along the signal leads in a balanced microphone cable, which means that no extra wiring is necessary. The same voltage is applied to both the hot and cold conductors, and isolating circuitry at the preamp input prevents the DC voltage from getting into the preamp's input stage. Similar components are used within capacitor microphones to isolate the phantom power from the audio signal.

Home Recording

There's no risk associated with connecting a dynamic mic to a phantom-powered input as long as the mic is wired for balanced operation and a balanced cable is used, but the mic could be damaged if it is unbalanced or used with an unbalanced cable. Nevertheless, if it's possible to switch off the phantom power for inputs that don't need it, you should do so. Figure 2.7 shows the schematic of a typical phantom powering system.

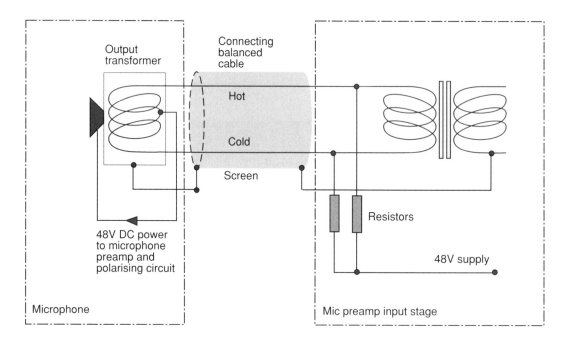

Figure 2.7: Phantom powering system

CARE AND FEEDING

Microphones are good investments as they don't go out of date and can last many years if looked after. Dynamic mics are the most rugged but should still be kept away from excessive moisture and dust, and they shouldn't be subjected to unnecessary physical shocks.

The same applies to capacitor mics, but these are even more susceptible to dust and moisture, to the extent that a singer with humid breath can cause a temporary change for the worse in the microphone's performance. A pop shield will help in this respect, as will working in a dry environment, and the mic should either be put away in its case or covered when not in use in order to prevent dust from creeping into the mechanism. If the mic is stored in a wooden case, don't slam the lid – this equates to an enormously loud sound and might just damage the diaphragm!

Home Recording

Time for another end-of-week test. This time,

everything you've learned about microphones over

the past week will be needed to answer the questions

below. Good luck!

1   Why is a cardioid pattern microphone so called?

2   What is the pickup pattern of an omnidirectional microphone?

3   Name two advantages of a capacitor microphone over a dynamic model.

4   Can phantom power be used with an unbalanced microphone or cable?

5   Why does a capacitor microphone need a power source?

6   What do you understand by a microphone having a built-in presence lift or

presence peak?

WEEK 3

RECORDING VOICES AND INSTRUMENTS

Even though there's still a little more theory to explore, I think it's time to get down to some practical recording, so this section deals with recording voices and instruments. As the vocals are the most important element of any song, I'll start there. To try this, you'll need a suitable microphone (ideally a capacitor model with a cardioid pickup pattern), a mic preamp or mixer that can provide 48V phantom power and a recording device, such as a MiniDisc recorder or a simple multitrack recorder (which could be a hardware device or a computer fitted with a suitable soundcard and music software). You'll also need a pop shield, a mic stand and some means of hearing the recording, which at its simplest will be a pair of headphones.

The pop shield is a simple but vitally important element of vocal recording. If you've ever tried to record vocals close to a mic without one, you'll probably have noticed that you occasionally get loud popping sounds on 'B' and 'P' sounds, known as *plosives*. On making these sounds, the mouth expels a strong blast of air which slams into the diaphragm of the mic, causing a loud, low-frequency noise that is almost impossible to remove after recording.

Pop shields should not be confused with the foam covers that sometimes come with microphones as part of their accessory kits. These covers offer little protection against popping (or anything else, for that matter) and often compromise the tonality of the mic by removing some of the high frequencies. A pop shield is simply a fine mesh screen, normally made from fine nylon stocking material stretched over

a plastic or metal hoop, and you can make your own with a cheap wooden embroidery hoop three or four inches in diameter. Commercial models come with a fitting that allows them to be attached to the same stand as the mic, but if you make your own, you may have to improvise a means of support. What's important is that the pop shield is positioned between the singer and the microphone at a distance of around two inches from the mic. The pop shield beaks up the blasts of air from the singer's mouth while not adversely affecting normal sounds.

When recording vocals, the mic should be between six and nine inches from the mouth, and the best results are often achieved with the mic an inch or two either above or below mouth level. If you can monitor the vocal sound using headphones as you fine-tune the mic position, you can decide exactly which mic position sounds most natural. Figure 3.1 shows a typical recording position for vocals.

Figure 3.1: Typical position for recording vocals with a pop shield

Home Recording

Before you start recording, you need to adjust the input gain on the mic preamp while the vocalist is belting out their loudest part. This will make sure that you get a healthy high signal level but will still give you a few decibels' safety margin before hitting maximum. You'll then need to adjust the output level of the preamp and/or the input gain of the recorder so that you also have an optimum level reading on the recorder's input level meter. Once these are set, you're ready to make a recording.

WHAT THE MIC HEARS

Although simply following the above steps will give you a reasonably faithful recording of what's in front of the microphone, the mic often 'hears' more than you want it to. For example, if you record the vocals in a bare room with a wooden floor, the reverberation and resonances of the room will contribute to the sound. If you're extremely lucky, you may find a room that actually improves the sound of singing by contributing a little reverberation, but more often than not you end up with a boxy, less than professional sound. Things improve in rooms that are fitted with carpets and soft furnishings, as these help to absorb the reflected sound that causes the colouration, but for the best results you may need to improvise a little acoustic treatment of your own. Fortunately, this is easy to do and needs no expensive equipment.

FIXING THE ACOUSTICS

If you're using a cardioid mic, the simplest way to set up for recording vocals is to place the mic well away from the walls of the room, so as to minimise reflections, but at the same time avoid placing it exactly in the centre of the room, as this can

emphasise the room's resonances. A couple of feet away from the centre of a typical room is fine. Because a cardioid mic picks up sound mainly from the front, it will also pick up any sound – including reflections – from behind the singer, so hanging some sound-absorbing material behind the singer can make a dramatic improvement. You could use acoustic foam or specially designed acoustic blankets, but a simple duvet or heavy sleeping bag makes a very effective acoustic screen, as shown in Figure 3.2. You should also avoid recording in very small spaces, as the sound can end up being very coloured and attempts to tame the environment using absorbers are less likely to be successful.

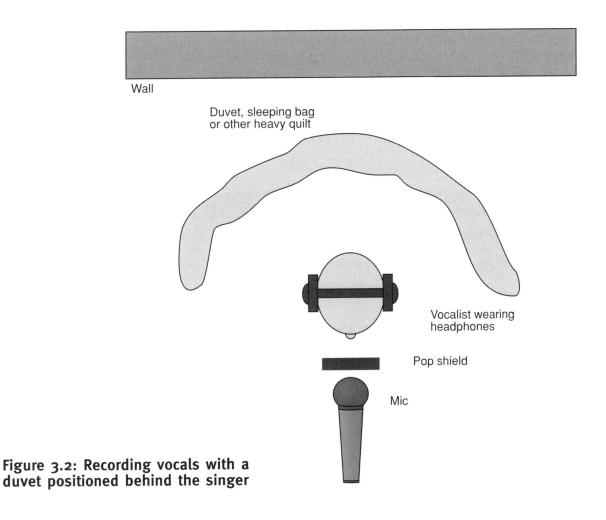

Figure 3.2: Recording vocals with a duvet positioned behind the singer

55

Home Recording

What you should hear when you play back your recording is a fairly 'dry' vocal sound, by which I mean it isn't significantly coloured by the sound of the room and has no audible reverberation. Of course, it won't be completely dry, but it should sound clean and natural. Studio recordings are made in a similarly acoustically dry environment, so some artificial reverberation may be added later. (This will be explained in Week 5, 'Effects And Processors'.) As *a cappella* vocal recordings are the exception rather than the rule, you'll probably apply these vocal techniques when working with multitrack or when recording a voice and an instrument at the same time. The same principle applies when singing over an existing karaoke backing track where a small mixer can be used to combine the backing track and the voice prior to recording.

THE PROS SAY...

Examine both the performances and your recording technique and see how you can get closer to the sound you're aiming for. Often this is as simple as moving the microphone or hanging up another sleeping bag.

ACOUSTIC INSTRUMENTS

Acoustic instruments are a little trickier to record, but still not difficult if you follow a few simple guidelines. Firstly, the better the instrument sounds in the room, the better the recording will sound, so try to find a room that's flattering to the instrument. For example, some of the biggest rock drum sounds are recorded in stone rooms or other very live environments, while orchestras and pianos are best recorded in a moderately reverberant concert-hall-type environment.

After vocals, one of the most popular instruments to record in the home studio is the acoustic guitar. Assuming you're recording in a moderately dry domestic room, you can liven up the sound of an acoustic a little by putting something hard and reflective – such as a sheet of MDF or plywood – on the floor beneath the recording position. If the instrument sounds OK to the player, you should be able to make a good recording.

A UNIVERSAL RULE

Most instruments have a 'loudest area' where you might instinctively think you should put the mic – for example, most of the sound from an acoustic guitar comes from the soundhole, brass and woodwind instruments emit a strong sound from the open end of the instrument, and so on. However, putting the mic close to this 'loud spot' invariably produces a less than accurate sound.

Virtually all acoustic instruments are more complex than you might imagine, and although they each have one spot that emits more sound than others, the sound that we hear in the room is actually a blend of all the sound emitted by all parts of the instrument. In order to capture this sound, the mic needs to be far enough away so as not to favour any one part of the instrument over another, and with this in mind I've devised a very simple rule for estimating the approximate minimum mic distance needed to get a good result.

Home Recording

TOP TIP

If you measure or estimate the longest dimension of that part of the instrument that emits sounds and then use that length as your mic distance, you'll have a good starting point. In the case of the acoustic guitar, the length of the guitar body works well as a ballpark mic distance, and in most cases you'll find that pointing the mic at the place where the neck joins the body gives an acceptable sound. However, the sound can change radically depending on the instrument and the room in which it is played, so the best results are obtained by monitoring the sound over headphones while you move the microphone around. Don't be afraid to experiment with the mic position, as this can make the difference between an OK recording and a brilliant one, and try to avoid pointing the mic directly at the soundhole of the guitar as this tends to produce a boomy or boxy sound. Even if you come across an instrument you've never recorded before, you can apply this principle to establish an approximate microphone distance. Figure 3.3 shows an acoustic guitar miked up in accordance with this principle.

VOICE AND GUITAR

Recording a singer who also plays the acoustic guitar can be very satisfying, and again it can be done using the minimum amount of equipment. You could simply use two mics, two mic preamps (or a dual preamp unit) and a stereo recorder, but if you do you'll end up with the voice mainly on one side of the mix and the guitar

Figure 3.3: Miking an acoustic guitar

mainly on the other, which isn't how you'd normally expect to hear it. You can make the recording in a more controlled way by using a small mixer to combine the voice and guitar signals and then use the mixer's pan controls to position the two sounds in the stereo mix; normally you'd expect to hear the voice in the centre of the mix and the guitar either in the centre or slightly to one side of the voice. If you have a reverb processor, you can also connect this to the mixer and add a little natural-sounding reverb while recording, as described in the sections on mixing.

Home Recording

The vocal and guitar mics can be set up as described earlier, but you can help

minimise the spill (ie the amount of guitar sound getting into the vocal mic, and

vice versa) by angling the mics so that the sound you don't want to pick up is in

the least sensitive area of the mic. Where cardioid mics are being used, this

means tilting the vocal mic upwards slightly and the guitar mic downwards. Figure

3.4 shows a typical microphone arrangement for recording guitar and voice.

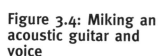 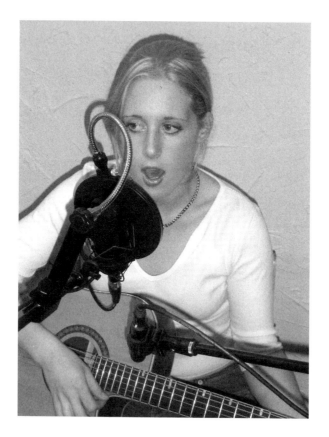

Figure 3.4: Miking an acoustic guitar and voice

It's possible to achieve even better separation between the vocals and the guitar

by using two figure-of-eight mics rather than cardioid models and aiming the

'deaf' side axis towards the sound being rejected. In this case, acoustic absorbers

are needed both behind and in front of the performer to prevent unwanted sounds from being picked up from behind the microphones, as figure-of-eight mics are just as sensitive at the rear as they are in front. Although this technique is too advanced to be covered in any kind of detail in this book, you should note that, no matter how carefully you position the microphones, there will be a significant amount of vocal picked up by the guitar mic and of guitar picked up by the vocal mic. However, this shouldn't be a serious problem as long as you have enough separation to allow you to achieve a natural balance between the two sounds.

DRUMS

It's quite a challenge to record drum kits properly, but it is possible to record them with a single microphone by applying the distance rule explained in the previous Top Tip. If you consider the drum kit as being a single instrument around five feet across, then the mic should be set up around five feet in front of the kit. Because you need to capture the high frequencies of the cymbals, capacitor mics are the preferred choice, and in most rooms cardioid models give the best results as they pick up little environmental acoustic influence. Set the mic up close to the ground to emphasise the kick-drum sound or move it higher to emphasise the cymbals. Even using a cardioid model, this one-mic technique works well, but only when the drum kit is being played in a room that flatters the sound; it's unsuitable for heavier pop and rock sounds, where individual drums tend to be close miked.

You can record the kit in stereo by placing two mics in front of the kit and spacing them by four or five feet. The left mic should be recorded onto the left recorder

Home Recording

track and the right mic onto the right recorder track. This technique can sound great for recording jazz music or any other genre where a very natural drum sound is needed. Both miking options are shown in Figure 3.5

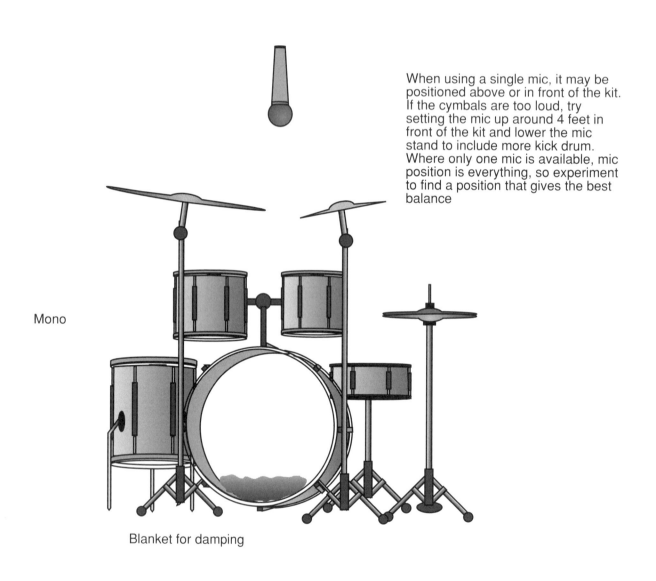

When using a single mic, it may be positioned above or in front of the kit. If the cymbals are too loud, try setting the mic up around 4 feet in front of the kit and lower the mic stand to include more kick drum. Where only one mic is available, mic position is everything, so experiment to find a position that gives the best balance

Mono

Blanket for damping

Figure 3.5a: Mono drum miking

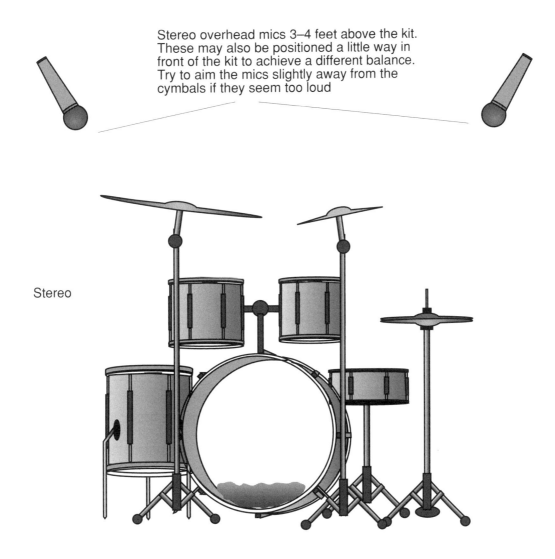

Stereo overhead mics 3–4 feet above the kit. These may also be positioned a little way in front of the kit to achieve a different balance. Try to aim the mics slightly away from the cymbals if they seem too loud

Stereo

Figure 3.5b: Stereo drum miking

If you have a mixer and more mics, you can gain more control over the overall balance of the kit by adding two dynamic mics, one for the snare drum and one for the kick drum. The snare mic should be positioned around two inches above the drum head and around two inches from the rim and should be angled to avoid

picking up too much hi-hat. The kick-drum mic needs to have a good bass response; a dedicated kick-drum mic will produce the deepest, most powerful sound.

For pop and rock work, the kick-drum mic should be positioned roughly in the centre of the drum shell, which means using a front drum head with a hole cut in it. The mic should be aimed at the spot on the rear head where the beater impacts, and folded blankets can be placed at the bottom of the drum to dampen unwanted ringing. The best sound is usually achieved by using the stereo capacitor mics to provide the main sound with the dynamic mics (panned centre) added as required to reinforce the kick and snare sounds. Figure 3.6 shows a drum kit miked with four microphones.

This four-mic technique is a good compromise between the minimalist mic technique described earlier and the professional method of miking the drum kit where further close mics are set up on each of the toms in much the same way as for the snare drum. There may also be a separate capacitor mic set up to capture the hi-hat, and some engineers also like to use a further mic beneath the snare drum, but that's getting rather too sophisticated for a book designed to introduce the basics! The main point to remember when combining close mics and a main pair of stereo mics is to pan the close mics so that their stereo positions match that of the main stereo pair. It's also common when close miking all the drums to increase the height of the stereo microphone pair so that they are two or three feet above the cymbals. (Mics set up above the drum kit are known, not surprisingly, as 'overheads'.)

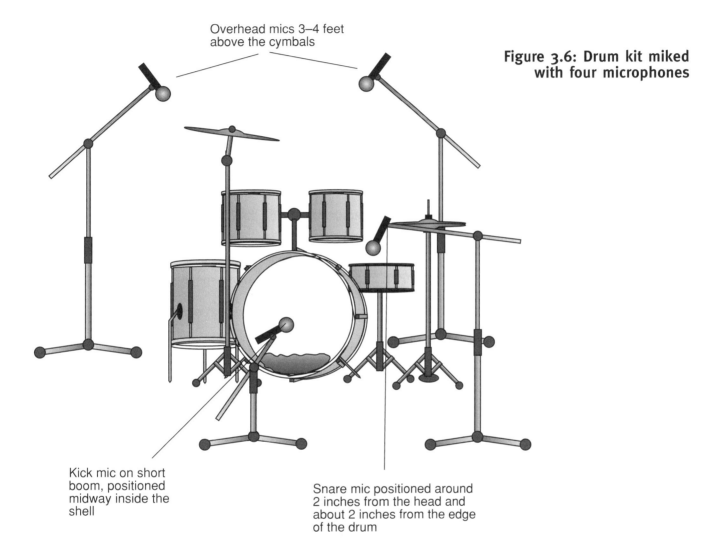

Overhead mics 3–4 feet above the cymbals

Figure 3.6: Drum kit miked with four microphones

Kick mic on short boom, positioned midway inside the shell

Snare mic positioned around 2 inches from the head and about 2 inches from the edge of the drum

When you first try to record a drum kit, avoid using EQ on the mixer and instead move the mics around if the sound isn't to your liking. Additional reverb can be added later if you're making a multitrack recording, and if you have enough tracks you can record each mic onto a separate track to give you greater flexibility when you come to mix.

Home Recording

ELECTRIC GUITARS

When it comes to recording, electric guitars are a special case as their sound depends on the instrument, on the amplification system and its loudspeaker, and on added effects such as distortion. Most guitar amps use 10- or 12-inch drivers without high-frequency tweeters in either sealed or open-backed cabinets. The distinctive overdrive sound is caused by harmonic distortion added in the amplifier and/or distortion pedal, which is then filtered by the limited frequency response of the speaker. Guitar speakers have an intentionally poor high-frequency response, which has the effect of filtering out the undesirable harmonics. If full-range hi-fi-style speakers were used, the overdrive sound would be rough and raspy. The guitar amplifier can be miked up to capture an authentic sound.

THE PROS SAY...

Famous studio saying: You can't polish a turd!

RECORDING USING A MICROPHONE

A general-purpose dynamic cardioid mic usually works fine, although a capacitor mic gives a brighter, more open sound that can work well with some musical styles. Guitar amplifiers aren't short on volume, so you don't need to worry about microphone sensitivity, and most good mics can handle the high SPLs (Sound Pressure Levels) involved. As a good guitar sound is subjective, any mic that sounds good is good!

Guitar amplifiers can be either close-miked (with the mic right up against the speaker grille), miked from a distance or even miked via a combination of both

methods by using two or more mics. Figure 3.7 shows a typical close-miked guitar combo.

Mic directed at the speaker from a position very close to the grille cloth. Move the mic to one side of the speaker opening for a less bright tone or move it further away from the grille cloth to allow the room acoustics to contribute to the sound

Note: Don't simply hang the mic in front of the cabinet by its cable as this will result in the mic's most sensitive axis pointing at the floor, which may lead to a duller tonality

Figure 3.7: Typical close-miked guitar combo

 TOP TIP

If the sound is too bright, don't simply reach for the EQ controls but instead try moving the mic. Aiming the mic at the centre of the speaker usually gives a brighter sound while moving it towards the edge of the speaker produces a warmer, less aggressive sound.

Home Recording

Like all performers, electric-guitar players respond to the sounds they are producing, and effects – particularly overdrive and delay – are often an integral part of the sound. The general rule is to leave adding effects until after recording, if at all possible, but with the electric guitar, effects such as overdrive and wah-wah should normally be recorded during the performance.

THE 5:1 RULE

Problems can arise when making a recording using multiple microphones as the finite speed of sound means that different sounds can reach different microphones at different times. These time delays are too short to hear as echoes, but they can adversely affect the overall audio quality when you come to mix, making the sound come across as muddy and confused. The way to minimise this problem is to make sure that the distance between the mics is at least five times greater than the distances between the mics and the sources they are recording, ensuring that the proportion of unwanted spill from other sources is kept down to acceptable levels. Apply the 5:1 rule wherever possible when recording acoustic ensembles, choirs, drum kits, vocalist/guitarists and so on. However, in situations where this is impractical, using directional microphones and aiming them appropriately can help to reduce spill from unwanted sources.

THE DI OPTION

Although recording with a mic is the most obvious way to capture the authentic electric-guitar sound, it's by no means the only approach. If you use a dedicated guitar-recording preamplifier, the guitar can be plugged straight into the recording

system without recourse to microphones at all. This is known as *direct injection*, or DI. Some of today's digital recording guitar preamps based on physical modelling (ie reproducing analogue sounds by digital means) are ideal for recording and have the ability to emulate the sounds of several classic amplifiers and effects pedals.

The DI approach has two main advantages: the guitarist hears the exact sound being recorded, and there's no noise to spill over onto other instruments or voices that are being recorded at the same time.

A simple DI box (a model with a high-impedance instrument input) may also be used to record the electric guitar, but this will result in a clean, clinical sound that may be fine for some rhythm sounds or other clean parts but doesn't actually sound like an amplified electric guitar. Nevertheless, for those using computer-based recording systems, there are software packages that can process a clean, DI'd part in much the same way as a digital-modelling guitar preamplifier. If these programs are used, it helps if the guitarist can hear the result in real time (in other words, while he's playing), as the sound will affect the way he plays.

OTHER INSTRUMENTS

The same miking rules can be applied to other instruments, but I can't emphasise too strongly that every situation is different, so be prepared to put on those headphones, listen and move the mic until you get the best result. If you do this – and also remain aware of the influence of the room's acoustics, improvising absorbers or screens where necessary – you'll be able to make truly excellent-

sounding recordings, as long as the quality of the performance matches your skill at recording. Professional engineers have the luxury of being able to try different mics, and it's true that different mics excel in different situations, but even when using a budget Far Eastern capacitor mic, you can get professional-sounding results if you take care and apply the basic rules.

The last point I'd like to stress is related to getting that great performance in the first place, and a big part of that is putting the performer at their ease, part of which comes down to providing them with a good monitor mix over their headphones. With singers, it's often helpful to add a little reverb, as this usually helps them with pitching, but always ask them what they want as some seem to like more reverb while others prefer to work with less.

THE PROS SAY...

Studio engineering isn't as glamorous as it's cracked up to be, especially if you're having to deal with inexperienced or emotionally unstable musicians.

The other important ingredient is you. Musicians are often nervous when recording, even if it's only in somebody's bedroom studio, so do your best to put them at ease and offer encouragement wherever you can. As most professional studio engineers have come to realise, having a good bedside manner can be as important as an ability to operate the equipment.

Home Recording

WEEK 3 TEST

Here's another test, this one designed to gauge your knowledge of getting a good recording sound. All of the answers were covered in the previous week. If you get stuck, check back and re-read the relevant sections until you feel you've fully understood the concepts involved.

1   Why should you always use a pop shield when recording vocals?

2   Why is it usually not best simply to aim a mic at the loudest point on an instrument?

3   How might you dampen down an acoustic environment that is too reflective or resonant-sounding?

Home Recording

4 If you are faced with the prospect of recording an unfamiliar instrument, what simple rule can you apply to estimate a suitable miking distance?

5 What do the letters DI stand for?

WEEK 4

MIXERS

Mixers are covered in more detail in my book *basic Mixers*, also available from SMT, but this chapter outlines the general principles, hopefully, without getting too technical. At the start of this book I introduced the concept of microphone preamplifiers, and a mixer can be thought of as two or more such preamplifiers, but also with line inputs and circuitry that allows their output signals to be mixed, controlled in level and routed to different destinations. Most mixers also include equalisation, which is also known as EQ, a fancy name for 'tone control'.

THE PROS SAY...

Never before have we had so much audio processing power available to us, but with power comes the ability to corrupt.

The other essential function of any recording mixer is to provide a separate level control for the studio monitor speakers or headphones, as well as some means of playing back a stereo recording over the speakers. Even if you need only a couple of mic preamps, a budget mixer might be the least expensive means of providing them.

In a recording context, a mixer provides the main means of routing signals to and from the recorder (which may or may not be a multitrack recorder) and also allows external effect and processor devices to be connected so that they may be used to treat signals passing through the mixer. Although big studio mixers can seem very complicated, with their rows of knobs and switches, all mixers are based on the principles introduced here and tend to be made up of several identical 'building blocks' known as *channels*.

Home Recording

THE MIXER CHANNEL

The purposes of a channel, in addition to doubling as a mic or line preamp, is to provide control over the level of the signal fed through it, to provide equalisation controls and to provide routing facilities so that the signal can be mixed with signals from other channels. On a mixing desk, controls and connections are also available to allow the channel signal to be processed using effects or processors.

The process of routing includes sending the channel signal to what is known as a *mix buss*, where it is mixed with the signals from the other channels. You can think of the buss (some people prefer to spell it 'bus') as a kind of audio-signal highway linking the various channels, and the place where the channel outputs are mixed. (On a very simple mixer where this is the only routing possibility, there may be no need for routing controls as all the channels always feed into the stereo mix buss.) The main mix busses then feed the output of the mixer, providing what's essentially a mixed signal (usually stereo), while other mix busses are often provided to feed effects units or studio monitoring systems.

A VERY BASIC MIXER

Whenever I'm asked to explain how mixers work, I invariably start off with a hypothetical four-channel model, as this is less daunting than a 48-channel studio console, even though the concept is exactly the same. If the mixer has four inputs but only one output, the output will be mono, which is of limited use. For stereo mixing, which is the format most recordists tend to work with, the mixer must have two main mix busses: one to carry the left signal and one to carry the right signal.

These signals are then recorded onto stereo media, such as CD or MiniDisc, and eventually feed the left and right speakers in a stereo replay system. A pan pot in each mix channel determines how much of the channel signal is fed to the left mix buss (and hence to the left output) and how much to the right.

PREAMPS

A typical mixer channel starts with the mic/line preamp, where incoming signals are brought up to the internal line level required by the mixer. Recording mixers need balanced mic inputs plus facilities for engaging phantom power for use with capacitor microphones or active DI boxes that are designed to be run on phantom power.

Line-level signals don't need to pass through the microphone amplifier, so mixer channels generally have a separate line input, but mic and line inputs usually share the same gain control, although normally only the line or mic input may be used at once. (Note that phantom power is never applied to the line input, only the mic input.)

Figure 4.1 shows a simplified schematic of a four-channel, stereo mixer with simple bass and treble (sometimes called 'high and low') equalisation. There are separate sockets for both microphone and line inputs, and on commercial mixers a switch is often – but not always – used to select between the mic input and the line input. Depending on the mixer's level of sophistication, there may also be a switchable low-cut filter (similar to that on some microphones) to reduce the level

Home Recording

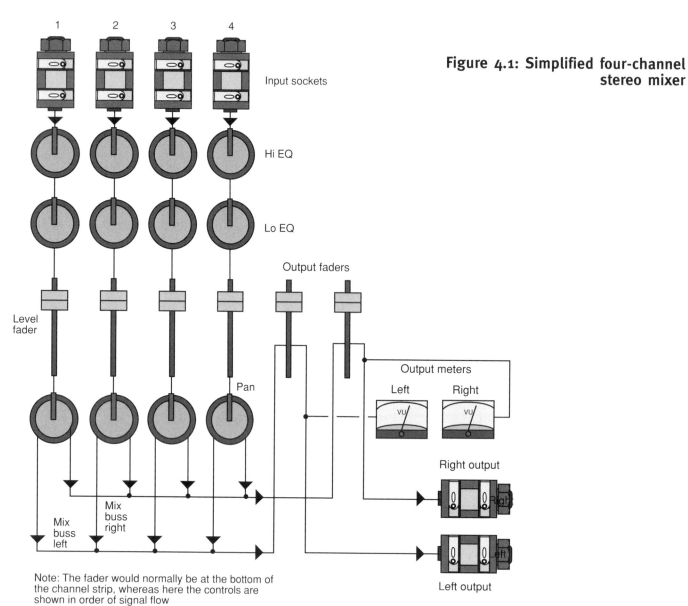

Input sockets

Hi EQ

Lo EQ

Output faders

Level fader

Pan

Output meters

Left   Right

Right output

Mix buss right

Mix buss left

Left output

Note: The fader would normally be at the bottom of the channel strip, whereas here the controls are shown in order of signal flow

Figure 4.1: Simplified four-channel stereo mixer

of unwanted low-frequency audio, such as traffic rumble or vibrations transmitted through the floor. A further button may be included to invert the phase of the input signal, but this is only relevant where multiple microphones are being used on the same sound source, a situation that's really beyond the scope of this book.

CHANNEL EQ

After the input-gain stage comes the EQ section, which is sometimes as straightforward as basic bass and treble controls, although there may be an additional switch allowing the equalisation section to be bypassed when not in use. All mixer EQ is arranged with a cut/boost control so that – for example – the high or treble control can be used to reduce the amount of treble as well as boost it. (Equalisation is discussed in a little more detail in Week 5, 'Effects And Processors'.) Where there isn't a bypass switch, the EQ cut/boost controls usually have a centre detent or click position that marks the point where the EQ has no effect (zero cut or boost).

Finally, the level of the channel signal is controlled by a knob or fader before feeding into the pan control, after which it's routed to the mix buss, sometimes via an On or Mute switch.

The combined signal on the two mix busses (usually referred to in the singular as the *stereo mix buss*) is controlled by a further master level fader or knob which adjusts the overall output level of the mixer. In a stereo mixer, there are actually two master faders, one for the left output and one for the right, although some models use a single physical control linking the two faders to save on cost and space. Our hypothetical mixer also includes a stereo-level meter that displays the output level of the mixer.

Home Recording

Note: A stereo mixer of this type is usually described as being a 'something into two' mixer, ie 12:2, where the '12' refers to the number of input channels and the '2' refers to the stereo output (left and right).

INSERTS AND AUX SENDS

All but the simplest mixers include what are known as *channel insert points*, which are simply sockets connected between each channel's mic amp and its EQ section (although in some mixers they may come after the EQ or be switchable pre- or post-EQ) to allow the channel signal to be processed via an external processing device, such as an equaliser, compressor or gate. These insert points are most often provided on TRS jacks (the same type of tip/ring/sleeve sockets used for stereo headphones) wired in such a way that, when no plug is inserted, spring contacts inside the socket complete the connection, allowing the signal to flow directly from the preamp section to the EQ section. In other words, if nothing is plugged into the socket, the signal flows as though the socket wasn't there, but when a suitably wired 'Y-type' TRS jack cable and external processor are connected, the preamp signal (the *insert send*) is diverted via the external processor before being returned (via the *insert return*) to the input of the EQ section. The external device is thus effectively inserted into the signal path between the preamp and EQ section. More sophisticated mixers may also have insert points in the main stereo output path, allowing the overall mix to be processed via an external (stereo) device. Figure 2.2 shows our four-channel mixer with both insert and aux sends added.

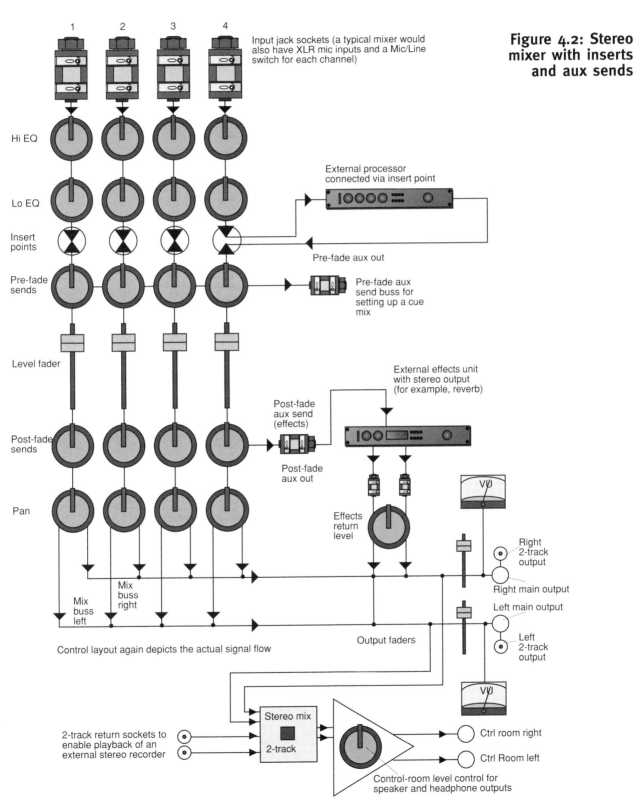

Figure 4.2: Stereo mixer with inserts and aux sends

Input jack sockets (a typical mixer would also have XLR mic inputs and a Mic/Line switch for each channel)

Hi EQ

Lo EQ

External processor connected via insert point

Insert points

Pre-fade aux out

Pre-fade sends

Pre-fade aux send buss for setting up a cue mix

Level fader

External effects unit with stereo output (for example, reverb)

Post-fade aux send (effects)

Post-fade sends

Post-fade aux out

Pan

Effects return level

VU

Right 2-track output

Right main output

Mix buss right

Mix buss left

Left main output

Left 2-track output

Control layout again depicts the actual signal flow

Output faders

VU

Stereo mix

2-track

Ctrl room right

Ctrl Room left

2-track return sockets to enable playback of an external stereo recorder

Control-room level control for speaker and headphone outputs

Home Recording

AUXILIARIES

Auxiliaries are used to create separate mixes in order to feed external effects devices such as reverb units, or to drive monitoring systems for performers who are overdubbing parts and need to hear what they've already recorded while playing or singing. In live performance, a cue mix is needed to feed stage monitor amplifiers.

There are actually two different types of auxiliary send, each with a different purpose: one for feeding effects and the other for setting up cue or monitor mixes. Mixers can have more than one of each type of send, but our simple four-channel mixer has just one of each. The pre-fade aux send is invariably used for setting up monitor mixes and is fed from the channel signal before the channel fader so that the channel fader doesn't affect it – any mix set up using the pre-fade aux send will be completely independent of the channel faders. Pre-fade send mixes are usually mono.

If you look at Figure 4.2, you can see both types of send, where the aux 1 control is simply another level control feeding a new mono mix buss running across the mixer

to the aux 1 master level control and then to the aux 1 output socket. The overall aux 1 mix level is set using the aux 1 master level control, although some very simple mixers omit this. In the studio, the engineer would normally use the pre-fade send to feed a headphone amplifier, thus providing the musician with a customised monitor mix that is independent of the main stereo mix.

The second aux control, aux 2, takes its feed from after the channel fader (ie *post-fader*), which means that its level will be affected by any changes in the channel-fader setting. The post-fade send is normally used to feed an effect unit, such as a reverb processor. Using a post-fader signal source means that, when the channel signal level is turned up or down, the amount of signal being sent to the effect unit changes by exactly the same amount, so the relative level of the effect remains constant. The output from the effect unit is added back into the mix via special inputs known as *aux returns* (really just simplified input channels), where it is added to the unprocessed (dry) signal on the main stereo mix buss.

By using different settings of the aux 2 control on each channel, it's possible to send different amounts of each channel's signal to the same effect unit and so regulate the amount of effect that's added to each of the sounds being mixed.

 An effect unit used in conjunction with a channel aux send should be set up so that it outputs only the effected sound and none of the original. This is usually accomplished by means of a Mix control, where the mix should be set to 100% effect, 0% dry.

Home Recording

TOP TIP

Where no dedicated aux return is provided, the effect may be fed into a spare input channel (or pair of channels panned hard left and right for stereo, in the case of reverb, which often has a mono input but a stereo output), although you must ensure that the corresponding aux send (in this case aux 2) is turned completely down on the channel or channels being used as returns or the effected signal will be fed back into the effect unit, causing screaming feedback! The mixer controls back in Figure 4.2 are arranged in the order of signal flow rather than in their more usual places on an actual mixer, where the fader is invariably right at the bottom of the channel.

MONITOR OUTS

Virtually all recording mixers have separate main outputs and monitor outputs, the essential difference being that the monitor outs go via a separate level control that can be used to turn the level of any connected speaker system up or down without affecting the main output level. There may also be a switching system allowing you to 'eavesdrop' on different signals (such as the various aux sends) within the mixer by listening in on them using the monitor output or the headphone output. This can be useful for checking levels when setting up prior to recording or mixing.

TAPE MONITOR

Although not shown on the mixer diagrams in Figures 4.1 and 4.2, the vast majority of mixers include a tape-monitor feature that allows the user to play back a stereo recording made on a tape machine or MiniDisc recorder via the mixer's monitor section. This is useful for checking a mix that you may have made on an external stereo recorder connected to the main outputs, or to a dedicated tape output, if available. Tape outputs – often called two-track outputs – carry an exact copy of the main stereo output, but usually via unbalanced phono connectors for straightforward connection to domestic recorders or sound systems.

When two-track or tape is selected as the playback source, the monitor output's normal stereo mix is replaced by the two-track/tape signal, whereas the main stereo mixer outputs remain unaffected. When 'left/right mix' is selected as the monitor source, the main mix is once again heard over the speakers.

EFFECTS AND PROCESSORS

While it is permissible to connect any type of effect or signal processor via a channel-insert point, there are restrictions on what can be used via the aux send/return system. As a rule of thumb, only delay-based effects such as reverb, echo, chorus, phasing, flanging and pitch shifting should be connected via the aux system, and these are what I will refer to as *effects*. If there's a dry/effect mix knob or parameter, the device is almost certain to be an effect, as it works by adding a treated signal (sometimes described as being *wet*) to an untreated (*dry*) signal.

Home Recording

A processor, such as an equaliser, gate or compressor, doesn't add to the original signal, but rather changes the whole of the original signal, hence processors are normally connected only via insert points.

MIXERS FOR MULTITRACKING

Mixers designed specifically for multitrack recording have a number of features that allow them to behave almost as two independent mixers: one for feeding signals into the various inputs of the recorder and another to mix the outputs from the recorder back into stereo. A multitrack mixer has additional output busses over and above the usual stereo mix buss, and each of these feeds one input of the multitrack recorder. However, you can use a much simpler mixer for basic multitrack recording, provided that you don't need to record too many parts at the same time – for example, a simple stereo mixer will allow you to record at least two parts at once via its main left and right outputs.

If you want to feed more recorder inputs simultaneously, you really need a mixer with additional output mix busses, but as most home recording is done by overdubbing one or two parts at a time, you can usually get by with a simpler, less expensive mixer.

THE PROS SAY...

Knowing how to use all these processors is essential to getting the best out of them, but perhaps even more important is the ability to know when to leave well alone – and that takes more experience than you might initially imagine!

A common mistake that even experienced users make is to refer to a mixer as having so many 'tracks'. Mixers don't have tracks, of course; they have channels (inputs) and outputs that may or may not be fed to the track inputs of a multitrack recorder.

PAN AND ROUTING

I don't want to focus too much on multitrack mixers here, as most of the techniques described in this book can be explored using a suitably chosen simple stereo mixer. Nevertheless, having a look here at the main features of a mixer designed for multitrack recording is a worthwhile exercise.

On each input channel, usually near the channel fader, there's a routing button for each additional pair of mix busses, with the pan control being used to 'steer' the channel signal between the odd- and even-numbered busses. For example, if you want to route a channel only to buss output 2, you'd press the routing button marked '1,2' and then turn the pan control fully clockwise so that the channel signal went only to buss output 2. You can route other channels in a similar way when you want to mix several signals together to record via buss output 2. A typical recording mixer might have eight additional output busses over and above the usual stereo buss, accessed by four additional routing buttons per channel.

HOW MANY BUSSES?

Of course, you don't have to use an eight-buss mixer to work with an eight-track recorder if you don't need to record all eight tracks at once. In fact, many budget

Home Recording

mixers have eight outputs for feeding a multitrack recorder, but these are fed from only four mix busses. How does this work? The output sockets feeding the multitrack inputs are wired so that output 1 feeds sockets 1 and 5, output 2 feeds sockets 2 and 6, and so on. The multitrack recorder's Record Ready buttons then determine which of the two possible tracks each output will record onto. The only limitation of using this method is that you can record a maximum of only four different tracks at a time.

RECORDING AND MONITORING

A dedicated mixer designed for multitrack recording has some channels designated for sending signals to the recorder and others for setting up a mix of the recorder's outputs, which is essential both for monitoring while overdubbing new parts and for mixing the final recording into stereo. There are ways to use a far simpler stereo mixer for recording, as will be explained shortly, although the best compromise is to use a mixer that has two or four additional buss outputs. This concept is easiest to explain by example, so first let's assume we're using an eight-track recorder.

Start by connecting the outputs of your multitrack recorder to the first eight channels of the mixer and routing these directly to the stereo L/R mix. This is your monitor section, where you'll balance the mix of existing recorded tracks so that the performers overdubbing new parts feel comfortable. You can use any remaining channels to handle the signals being recorded, which are routed to the recorder via the buss-routing buttons, with the number of busses at your disposal determining how many different parts you can record at the same time. Working this way, you can build up your mix, and monitor it with added effects, as you record.

Once all the tracks have been recorded, you can mix the eight tracks and record the result to a stereo recorder. Figure 4.3 shows how this system is connected up.

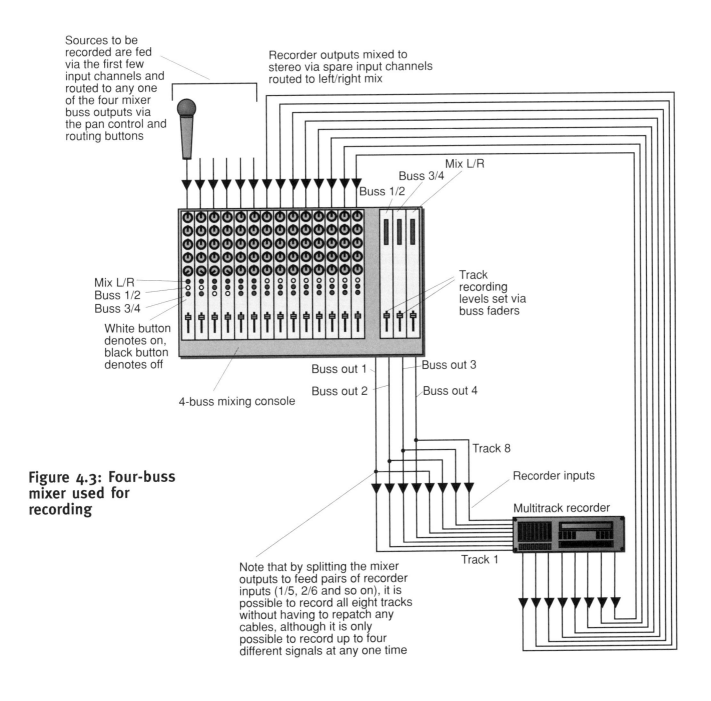

Sources to be recorded are fed via the first few input channels and routed to any one of the four mixer buss outputs via the pan control and routing buttons

Recorder outputs mixed to stereo via spare input channels routed to left/right mix

Mix L/R

Buss 3/4

Buss 1/2

Mix L/R
Buss 1/2
Buss 3/4

White button denotes on, black button denotes off

Track recording levels set via buss faders

4-buss mixing console

Buss out 1
Buss out 2

Buss out 3
Buss out 4

Track 8

Recorder inputs

Multitrack recorder

Figure 4.3: Four-buss mixer used for recording

Track 1

Note that by splitting the mixer outputs to feed pairs of recorder inputs (1/5, 2/6 and so on), it is possible to record all eight tracks without having to repatch any cables, although it is only possible to record up to four different signals at any one time

Home Recording

SOUNDCARD STUDIOS

If you're using a computer-based recording system, a simple hardware stereo mixer provides an ideal, cost-effective way of recording up to two parts at the same time and also of controlling your monitor level. Simply use the main stereo outputs to feed the inputs to the soundcard and connect the soundcard outputs to the two-track input of the mixer. Next, switch the mixer's monitor source to '2-track'. In effect, this separates the mixer into two parts, where the channels and main stereo outputs take care of signals being recorded and the monitor section of the mixer 'listens' to the outputs of the soundcard and then sends them to your speakers and headphones. (Most music software has built-in mixing facilities, and so a stereo soundcard output is all that's needed.) It's worth repeating that, because the mixer is in two-track monitoring mode, the control-room monitor section is completely isolated from rest of the mixer, which in any event is being used simply as a convenient source of mic preamps. When used in this way, the mixer never actually does any mixing, but it's still a vital part of the system!

DIGITAL MIXERS

Digital mixers do essentially the same job as their analogue counterparts, the main practical difference being the user interface, on which many of the functions – including such things as fader levels, pan settings and aux-send levels – can be automated using either a built-in or computer-based automation system that records your fader and control moves. Many of these mixers have motorised faders that move according to the automation data you have stored.

The signal flow is similar to that of the analogue mixers described earlier, but to save on cost and panel space there are far fewer physical controls, with often only one set of EQ controls shared between all of the mixer channels. It's much easier to use a digital mixer if you already know your way around an analogue mixer, although any further discussion of digital mixers is rather beyond the remit of this book. To learn more about mixers and mixing, see my book *Home Recording Made Easy* (second edition), also published by SMT.

TOP TIP

If your mixer has a pre-fade send that you're not using for any other purpose, you can use it to record an additional signal at the same time as the signals feeding the stereo output. In other words, you can record three tracks at a time rather than two. To do this, turn the fader right down on the channel used to feed the third track and then use its pre-fade send to route the channel signal to the pre-fade send output. By connecting this pre-fade send output to the multitrack recorder input you want to record to, you can record it independently of the other two outputs and the record level can be set using the pre-fade master send level, if fitted, or using the channel pre-fade send control if no master control is available. Figure 4.4 over the page shows this simple but highly effective way of working.

Home Recording

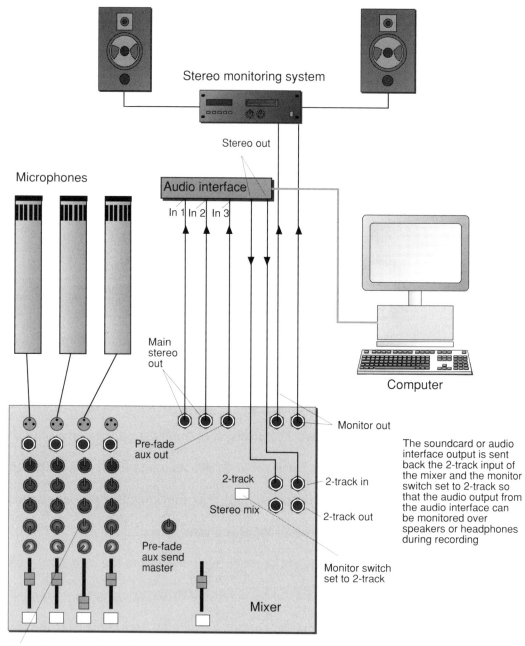

Stereo monitoring system

Stereo out

Microphones

Audio interface

In 1 In 2 In 3

Computer

Main
stereo
out

Monitor out

Pre-fade
aux out

The soundcard or audio
interface output is sent
back the 2-track input of
the mixer and the monitor
switch set to 2-track so
that the audio output from
the audio interface can
be monitored over
speakers or headphones
during recording

2-track

2-track in

Stereo mix

2-track out

Pre-fade
aux send
master

Monitor switch
set to 2-track

Mixer

Pre-fade aux send is used as an extra means to send a signal from the mixer by turning
the channel fader down and the pre-fade aux send control up. The pre-fade send output
feeds the third input on the audio interface or soundcard. The first two channels are sent to
soundcard inputs 1 and 2 via the mixer's main stereo outputs using the pan controls to
send channel 1 to the left output and channel 2 to the right output

Figure 4.4: Using a stereo mixer to record three tracks in a soundcard studio

Home Recording

Now it's time for another test to consolidate the welter of information you (hopefully) picked up over the previous week. Again, if any of the following seems unclear, go back and re-read the relevant section until you understand things better.

1   If you wish to connect an effect that can be applied to all the mixer channels but to varying degrees, would you connect it to:

A   An insert point?

B   An aux send/return loop?

C   A mic input?

2   If a mixer is described as being a 32:2 format, how many input channels does it have?

How many outputs does it have?

Home Recording

3 A mixer has four additional mix busses over and above the usual main left/right buss, each buss pair being addressed by a single routing button. These buttons are labelled 'left/right', '1/2' and '3/4'. How would you route a channel signal to buss 3?

4 In a simple 12:2 mixer, how many controls can be used to adjust the level of the channel 1 signal before it reaches the main stereo output sockets? What are they called?

WEEK 5

EFFECTS AND PROCESSORS

In the previous week, I made a distinction between effects and processors, and this gave us some simple guidelines concerning connected them to a mixer, whether hardware or software. Delay-based effects – such as reverb, echo, chorus, phasing, flanging and pitch shifting – may be connected either via the mixer's post-fade aux/return system or via one of the mixer's insert points.

TOP TIP

If the device (or software plug-in) has a dry/effect mix knob or parameter, it is almost certainly an effect.

The advantage of connecting via the effects send/return system is that the same effect may be added to any of the mixer channels in different proportions, with the amount of effect added being set by the channel aux-send knob.

TOP TIP

When an effect is fed from a post-fade aux send and back into the mixer via the return inputs (or via spare mixer channels), the mix parameter must be set to 100% effect, 0% dry sound. The necessary dry sound comes via the mixer channel, as usual, so all you need to add is pure effect.

Home Recording

Where the mixer has more than one post-fade aux-send control, additional effect units may be connected up. For example, some engineers like to have a short reverb available for drums and other instruments and a longer reverb for vocals, requiring the use of two reverb units. These are invariably connected via the mixer's aux send/return system, rather than via insert points, as it's common to use reverb on many different tracks within a mix. Also, each reverb unit has a stereo output, which can't be used when the unit is connected via a mono insert point. Where effects are used via insert points, only the signal passing through that insert point can be treated.

In contrast, processors – including compressors, gates, equaliser, expanders, limiters and many types of psychoacoustic enhancer or exciter – are usually used only via the mixer's insert points or via other configurations where the entire signal can be fed through them. Other than some types of enhancer, they have no wet/dry mix control. If you tried to use a processor in the effect send/return loop, you'd risk adding the processed signal to the dry signal, which tends to produce unpredictable and undesirable results.

 Sometimes you can get around a limitation imposed by the routing shortcomings of your mixer by feeding a processor from a pre-fade send and then muting the dry signal. However, until you're more familiar with signal routing, sticking to the 'inserts only' rule will help you to avoid problems.

SOFTWARE OR HARDWARE?

Originally, all effects and processors were external hardware boxes, but today we can also buy analogue mixers with built-in effects, digital mixers with both built-in effects and processors, and of course software plug-ins for use with audio software. However, the way in which these effects and processors work, and the way in which they are connected and used, is pretty much the same regardless of the format in which they appear. This week I'll be covering the most commonly used studio effects and including a brief description of the applications of each.

THE PROS SAY...

On a practical level, when you strip away the user-interface differences, both the hardware and software studio user are ultimately working with the same basic tools.

REVERBERATION

Reverberation – or reverb for short – is the most important studio effect and is an essential tool used to reintroduce a sense of space and place into recordings made in an acoustically 'dry' or small-sounding environment, such as a home studio. Reverberation occurs naturally when sound is reflected and re-reflected from walls and other obstacles within a room or other acoustic space, and an electronic reverb unit mimics this effect by generating thousands of reflections electronically. Figure 5.1 shows the pattern of decaying reflections created by a typical digital reverberation unit.

These reflections very quickly become denser and more complex, but they also decay in level as the sound energy is absorbed by the air and surfaces in the

Home Recording

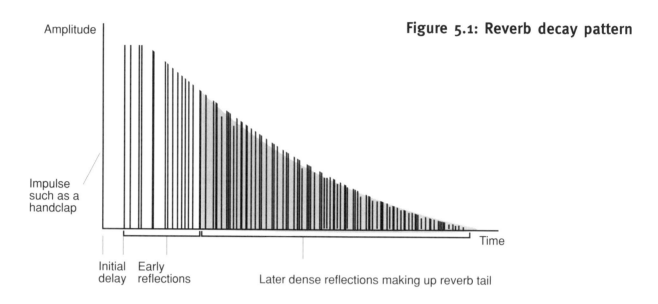

Figure 5.1: Reverb decay pattern

room. The first part of the reverberant sound, where some individual reflections may be audible, is known as the *early reflections phase*, while the denser decay following it is known as the *reverb tail*. Rooms with hard surfaces produce a bright, lively reverb sound while more absorbent rooms produce a warmer sound with much less high end.

CONVOLUTION

Most reverb units synthesise these reflections electronically, but a newer breed of reverb processor based on a mathematical process known as *convolution* enables the acoustic characters of real rooms (and of other hardware or software reverb devices) to be captured using special test signals and then recreated digitally in the studio. In theory, you can add the sonic characteristic of a world-class concert hall or top-shelf electronic reverb unit to your music using one of

these devices. At the time of writing, the most affordable convolution-based reverb units are software-based models and tend to use much more processing power than synthetic reverberation.

ROOM SIMULATION

Although a typical reverb device comes with a variety of presets, including settings emulating caverns, cathedrals and large rooms, most musical applications require fairly short reverb times, of between one and three seconds, although longer reverb times are useful for creating special effects. Plate and chamber settings work well on most musical sound sources, including vocals and drums. (The term *plate* refers here to the mechanical reverb plate that was used in studios before the advent of digital reverb units.) Some units can also emulate the sound of the spring reverb effect used in guitar amplifiers.

MONO IN, STEREO OUT

The vast majority of reverb units generate a stereo output regardless of whether the input is mono or stereo. Indeed, most mix the two stereo signals into mono before feeding this signal into the reverb processor, although the dry sound fed to the mix control always remains in stereo. The reason for having a stereo output is that, in a real acoustic space, each ear picks up a slightly different pattern of reverb reflections because the ears are in different physical locations within the space of the room. This difference in the aural signal is what creates the perception of stereo width.

TOP TIP

Digital reverb units create two different sets of synthetic reflections from a mono source in order to create a stereo spatial effect. This means that you need to feed the reverb unit from a mono post-fade aux send and return it to a stereo aux return (or to two mono returns panned left and right, respectively).

REVERB PARAMETERS

Even though you can simply call up a preset emulating a room, hall or plate, most reverb units allow the user to edit the effect further to some extent, ranging from simply adjusting the decay to changing dozens of separate variables. However, the main reverb parameters are pre-delay time, early-reflection pattern, overall decay time and high-frequency dampening, while it may also be possible to adjust the relative levels of the early reflections and the reverb tail. The pre-delay setting adjusts the time between the original sound and the first reverb reflection and provides one simple way of creating the illusion of room size. Longer pre-delays often sound effective when treating vocals, with 80ms being a typical value.

The reverb decay time – which is another way of saying how long the reverb takes to die away – also affects the perceived size of the environment. Longer reverb times suggest large, reflective spaces while shorter decay times are used to emulate smaller rooms or plates. Patterns of early reflections with little or no tail may also be used to add ambience and space to a sound without adding any obvious reverb.

High-frequency dampening adjusts the high-frequency decay time independently of the low-frequency decay time. The greater the HF dampening, the faster the high frequencies decay relative to the low frequencies. This is what you hear in a room where there are soft furnishings or carpets, as these soak up high-frequency energy more than they do low-frequency energy. Large rooms also exhibit high-frequency dampening due to the way in which air absorbs sound.

EARLY REFLECTIONS

The pattern of early reflections is what gives a room or other space its sonic signature. These early reflections are audible for only a very short time following the initial sound, after which the reverb pattern becomes increasingly more dense and homogenised. The various presets emulating rooms, plates, halls, caverns and so on each have their own early-reflections pattern, which can be either synthesised (in the case of conventional electronic reverb) or taken from a real-life space (in the case of a convolution reverb).

THE PROS SAY...

If the unprocessed recording doesn't sound pretty good in the first place, then it's probably not good enough to use.

By selecting the basic room type and then adjusting its parameters, it's possible to recreate almost any imaginable acoustic space, from a barely perceived ambience to a cavernous reverb that rolls on for ten seconds or more. Be aware, however, that convolution reverbs have far fewer user-adjustable parameters, as they are, in effect, recreating the acoustic of a real-life environment.

Home Recording

GATED AND REVERSE REVERB

Most reverb devices include gated and reverse reverb options, which, although not recreations of anything natural, can be used creatively in mixing. Gated reverb is characterised by an abrupt cut-off rather than a smooth decay and is created by a burst of closely spaced reflections of similar level that stop abruptly after around half a second. The effect was first developed for use on drums, where it can create a big, exciting sound without filling up all the important spaces with reverb tail.

Reverse reverb is similar to gated reverb except that the level of the burst of reflections starts off low and then increases steadily, producing an effect not unlike that of a tape being played backwards. With gated and reverse reverb, the main parameter is the length of the reflections burst.

USING REVERB

As a rule, reverberation makes a sound appear more distant, so it's best not to overuse it when you want a sound to appear to be at the front of a mix. For this reason, most vocal reverb treatments are fairly short and bright, featuring typically no longer than two seconds of decay time. It's also advisable not to add much in the way of reverb to bass sounds or kick drums as it can blur the low end of a mix. If reverb is needed in these areas, short room or ambience treatments usually work best. Unless you specifically want the reverb to be audible as an effect, you should add just enough to make the recording sound as though it was made in a real room and not in a dead studio. Of course, mixing is an art in itself, so any of these guidelines can be broken if you think the result sounds right.

ECHO

Echo effects are based on the principle of delaying a sound and then feeding some of the delayed sound back into the input to create repeating echoes that gradually die away. Echo units were originally based on tape loops, but now most are digital. The time it takes for the echoes to die away is adjusted via the Feedback control.

The old tape-based echo units often had three or four playback heads to give a more complex pattern of echoes, and this can be emulated digitally by simultaneously setting up several different delay times, or 'taps'. It may also be possible to pan the individual delays from left to right, which is something tape echoes didn't offer. Again, the Feedback parameter determines how many repeats are created and how quickly they die away.

Hardware delay units often have a manual 'tap tempo' feature, which allows you to match the delay time to the song tempo by tapping in time on a button two or three times. Software delays often go one better and allow you to match the delay time to the song tempo automatically.

Echo has always been a popular effect on electric guitar, from surf bands to Pink Floyd, and on some types of vocals, right back from the early days of rock 'n' roll. Used creatively, however, it can be applied to almost any sound. Very short delays with little or no feedback are also useful for thickening or doubling vocals.

Home Recording

MODULATED DELAY

A simple delay unit can be made to produce a wider range of effects if a low-frequency oscillator (similar to the one used in guitar-amp vibrato circuits) is used to modulate (which simply means vary) the delay time. Modulating the delay time creates a wavering-pitch effect that can be used to generate effects such as chorus, flanging, vibrato and phasing. All the common modulation effects are created using LFO modulation by juggling the delay time, the wet/dry mix and the amount of feedback.

As the majority of effect units now come with presets to bring about these basic effects, there's no need to go into too much detail about their actual settings, but I encourage you to experiment with the presets rather than just accept them as they are. Your ears will tell you what's right and what isn't, because if the modulation depth is too high or the rate too fast, the sound takes on an unnatural warbling characteristic. As a rule, the faster the modulation rate, the less depth you need.

CHORUS

Chorus is one of the most popular modulation effects and has been used on countless guitar tracks. It was also a key ingredient in the original string-machine sound as it creates a passable illusion of ensemble playing, especially if two or more choruses are added together, each running at a slightly different rate. (Some chorus presets offer a multitap option which does much the same thing.)

ADT (Automatic Double Tracking) is similar to chorus but uses a slightly longer delay time and very gentle modulation to create a more natural doubling effect. Used on vocals, ADT can make it sound as if the same singer has performed the part twice, on different tracks, and again produces a thicker sound. Indeed, recording a part twice on two different tracks is how natural double tracking is achieved.

THE PROS SAY...

Don't simply assume that effects with presets will always sound right. In reality, each situation is slightly different.

PHASING

Phasing uses a fairly short delay of between one and ten milliseconds, featuring modulation and an equal mix of wet and dry sound. This arrangement creates a moving comb filter (a filter with deep notches in its frequency response) that adds movement to a sound without being too obtrusive. Phasing is a popular guitar effect but can also work well on keyboard pad sounds.

FLANGING

Flanging is similar to phasing but combines slightly longer delay times (up to 50ms) with feedback to create a very dramatic and instantly recognisable sweeping or whooshing effect. The further the Feedback control is advanced, the stronger the effect, while slower modulation rates produce the most effective sweeping sound. Phasing was introduced back in the era of psychedelic music, back in the late '60s, and works best on harmonically complex sounds. As it's such a dramatic effect, it's best not to overuse it!

Home Recording

VIBRATO

Vibrato is a straightforward modulation of pitch and is created by adding just enough modulation to the delayed sound to create the desired effect. The length of the delay used in vibrato is just a few milliseconds – a modulation rate of between two and seven cycles per second is typical – and so isn't perceived as being a delay at all. Vibrato can be used on any guitar or keyboard sound, although a rotary-speaker effect, which combines both level and pitch modulation, may sound more musically pleasing on some sounds.

PITCH SHIFTING

Pitch shifters are designed to change the pitch of a signal without making it sound faster or slower. They work by first breaking the sound into very short segments and then processing these individually, a process that can impart an unnatural modulation to the sound, making it sound slightly off-key. There's also a slight delay incurred by the looping process, but this can be as short as just a few milliseconds.

Smaller shifts in pitch (plus or minus around one-tenth of a semitone) sound very similar to chorus effects, but without chorus's characteristic regular pulse. Higher levels of shift can be used to generate parallel harmonies or octaves, but the greater the amount of shift, the more noticeable the side-effects are likely to be. Personally, I prefer to use pitch shifting only for creating chorus or thickening effects, although they may also be used to create sub-octave guitar parts and similar effects.

AUTOPANNERS

An autopanner pans a mono signal back and forth from left to right in the mix, usually under the control of a low-frequency oscillator or external trigger, and software autopanners are usually able to lock to a multiple of the song tempo. Because the effect can be fairly dramatic, it's best to use autopanning sparingly rather than applying it all the way through a song. Try it on a keyboard pad or on an effect such as delay or reverb.

AMP/SPEAKER SIMULATORS

Guitar and bass amplifiers are *voiced*, which means that their frequency response is shaped to suit the instrument. In general, the loudspeakers and enclosures used in guitar and bass amplifiers have a fairly limited frequency response, so if you wanted to plug a guitar directly into a recording system and have it sound as though it's played through an amplifier, the characteristics of both the amplifier and speaker would need to be replicated.

Both hardware and software guitar-amp emulators are available, most offering a choice of amplifier and speaker types. The best of these produce a sound almost indistinguishable from a professional electric-guitar recording and are often the best option in the home studio.

DISTORTION

Various devices and software plug-ins are available that distort sound, either by simulating analogue tape or tube saturation and clipping, or by reducing the bit

depth of the original audio signal. Digital distortions sound pretty nasty but are popular in dance music for creating 'lo-fi' sounds or 'grunging up' drum loops. Excessive use of distortion can cause the sound to become rough or ragged, although using EQ or filtering after the distortion to cut some of the high end can improve things in this respect. Guitar distortion pedals can be surprisingly effective in livening up tame bass-synth sounds.

FILTERS

There are effects that emulate the swept resonant filters used in synthesisers, and these may be controlled via an LFO, via the level of the input signal, or sometimes via their own MIDI-triggered envelope. Any audio signal can be treated, from basic keyboard sounds to drums and vocals, although the filter effect may be unpredictable when complex or polyphonic sounds are being processed. My advice? Try it and see!

PROCESSORS

Processors include exciters/enhancers, equalisers, compressors, limiters, gates, expanders, auto-panners and anything else that processes the entire signal, and as I explained earlier, this means that they are normally connected via your mixer's insert points. Processors shouldn't normally be used in the effects send/return loop, where the dry signal is combined with the processed signal.

COMPRESSOR/LIMITERS

If reverb is the most important effect, compression is definitely the most important processor. A compressor is a type of automatic gain-control device that 'evens out'

Too many effects? If you're looking for one button to make everything sound better, may I suggest Bypass?

excessive peaks in signal level that occur in vocal or instrumental performances. It works in much the same way as an engineer with his hand on the fader. If something is too loud, the engineer turns it down for a moment. In a compressor, this is achieved by the user setting a threshold above which signals will be deemed too loud and turned down, or compressed, accordingly. Below this level, the signal is left alone.

The amount of gain reduction applied during compression is determined by the Ratio control. The higher the ratio, the more the signal level is 'squashed' once it exceeds the threshold level. The input/output graph of a compressor is shown in Figure 5.2.

Figure 5.2: Graph showing soft- and hard-knee compression

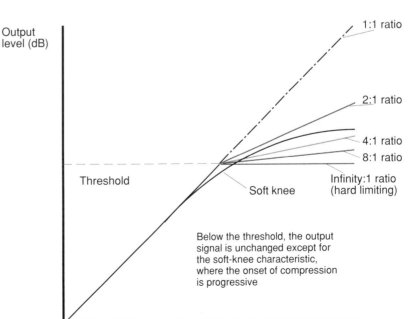

Output level (dB)

1:1 ratio

2:1 ratio

4:1 ratio

8:1 ratio

Threshold

Soft knee

Infinity:1 ratio (hard limiting)

Below the threshold, the output signal is unchanged except for the soft-knee characteristic, where the onset of compression is progressive

Input level (dB)

Home Recording

TOP TIP

The ratio of a compressor simply states the number of decibels by which the input must rise to cause a 1dB increase in output level when the threshold is exceeded. For example, a compression ratio of 4:1 means that a 4dB rise in signal above the threshold will result in a rise in output level of just 1dB.

Because heavy compression can reduce the overall level of a signal, an output gain control is usually provided to 'make up' any lost level. If the ratio is infinite, the compressor's maximum output is prevented from exceeding the threshold in a process known as *limiting*, used when there's a need to prevent a signal from ever exceeding a specific level – for example, to prevent clipping on a digital recorder.

A compressor's attack parameter determines how quickly the gain-reduction circuitry responds once a signal has exceeded the threshold, while the release setting determines the time it takes for the gain to return to normal once the input has dropped back below the threshold. Some compressors have an Auto setting that responds to the dynamic character of the input signal so that the user doesn't have to adjust the release time manually. As well as being convenient, Auto mode is also very useful for processing signals with constantly changing dynamics, such as complex mixes.

The part of the compressor that 'listens' to the incoming signal in order to decide how loud it is at any given time – known as the *side chain* – generates a control signal that tells the gain-control circuit what to do. Stereo compressors have two separate signal channels and their side-chain circuits are linked to ensure that both channels are always compressed by the same amount. This is necessary to prevent the image from appearing to move to one side or the other when a loud sound appears only on one side of a mix.

If you come across a compressor described as being 'soft knee', this simply means that its compression ratio increases gradually as the signal approaches the threshold level rather than starting suddenly, as is the case with a conventional or 'hard-knee' compressor. Soft-knee compressors tend to sound less obtrusive than hard-knee types, but they often don't offer such assertive gain control. The characteristic of a soft-knee compressor is also shown in Figure 5.2.

Compression is most useful on vocals, where it is an essential ingredient in getting the vocal line to sit in the mix at a constant level, and the better control the singer has, the less compression will be necessary. It's also useful in thickening and evening out drum sounds and bass instruments. Complete mixes may also be compressed to increase their average energy level and to make them sound louder. The vast majority of compressors have gain-reduction meters that show by how much they are turning down the level of your loud notes or phrases, and adjustments to the threshold are usually made while watching this meter. Ideally,

low-to-medium-level sounds should undergo little or no compression, with the loud peaks showing a maximum gain reduction of between 4dB and 8dB.

GATES AND EXPANDERS

Gates are almost the polar opposite of compressors as they turn down only quiet sounds. Their purpose is to silence the signal during pauses, when any background noise will not be masked by its presence. If the gate threshold level is set just above the background noise, the gate will operate whenever there is a pause in the signal, thus ensuring complete silence.

From this brief description, it's evident that gates remove noise only when there is a pause in the wanted signal – they can't help with noise that's audible over the top of wanted audio material. An Attack Time control may be provided on a gate to determine how fast it opens when the signal exceeds the threshold and a Release Time control will determine how quickly the gate closes down once the signal has fallen back below the threshold. The Release Time control is particularly important, as without it the gate may close too abruptly and chop off the end of a gradually fading or decaying sound.

Expanders are very similar to gates except that they attenuate the signal more progressively, more like a compressor in reverse. To accomplish this, they have an additional Ratio control.

EQUALISERS OR TONE CONTROLS?

Whatever anyone tells you to the contrary, equalisers (EQs for short) are just fancy tone controls! Most mixers have built-in EQ facilities, but you can also buy separate hardware EQs or software plug-ins. Equalisers come in all levels of complexity, but the most common are shelving and parametric EQs.

SHELVING EQUALISERS

A shelving equaliser applies cut or boost, rather like a volume control, but only to those frequencies above or below its so-called cutoff frequency (the frequency at which the filter is told to start working). On some models this may be variable by the user.

A low-pass shelving filter passes all frequencies below its cutoff frequency but attenuates (ie reduces the levels of) all frequencies above its cutoff frequency, while a high-pass filter passes all frequencies above its cutoff frequency but affects all frequencies below its cutoff frequency.

Figure 5.3 shows the frequency-response graphs of a typical high/low EQ based around high- and low-pass shelving filters. You'll notice that there isn't a sudden step at the cutoff point but a smooth slope, indicating a transition from no cut or boost to maximum cut or boost. Although it's technically possible to create a very sharp digital filter with an almost infinitely sharp response, it wouldn't sound very musical.

Home Recording

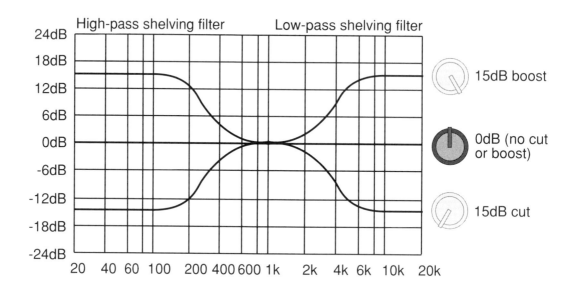

Figure 5.3: Shelving equaliser frequency response

The steeper the slope, the sharper the filter response is said to be, and the slope usually goes up in multiples of 6dB per octave as that's how analogue filters are constructed. Simple shelving filters typically have a gentle 6dB-per-octave slope, although steeper 12dB-, 18dB- and 24dB-per-octave slopes are also common. This type of shelving filter is often used for simple bass and treble adjustment where both cut and boost is available. The Cut/Boost control's central position is said to be 'flat', which simply means that no cut or boost is applied.

BAND-PASS FILTERS

A filter that passes frequencies between two limits is known as a *band-pass filter*, and on many mixers the Mid control is a band-pass filter, where the filter's centre frequency can also be adjusted using a separate control. Figure 5.4 shows a

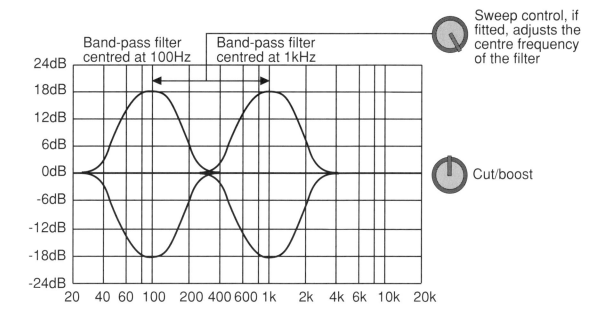

Figure 5.4: **Sweep equaliser frequency response**

typical band-pass filter response, including sweep-control function. Sweep equalisers have the advantage that they can be tuned to the exact frequency that needs cutting or boosting.

PARAMETRIC EQ

A parametric EQ is very similar to a sweep EQ, except it will have a third control that allows the width of the filter to be adjusted. This enables the user to focus in on a very narrow part of the audio spectrum, often as narrow as a single semitone. Conversely, a wide setting allows a broad area of the audio spectrum to be adjusted at once.

Home Recording

The width of a filter response may be specified as its *Q* value (the higher the Q,

the narrower the filter), or it may simply be specified as bandwidth, measured in

Hertz. Figure 5.5 shows the frequency response of a typical parametric equaliser.

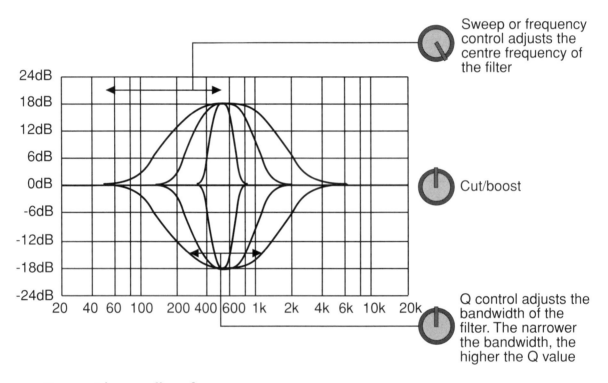

Figure 5.5: Parametric equaliser frequency response

EQ has both creative and corrective applications, but it always pays to get the

sound as good as possible at source and then use as little EQ as you can get away

with. However, EQ can be useful in trimming away low frequencies from some

sounds in a congested mix. For example, acoustic guitars and synth pads may sit

better in the mix and conflict less with other sounds if their low end is reduced in

level. A high-pass or low-cut shelving filter is usually fine for this application.

TOP TIP

It takes some practice to set up a parametric equaliser properly, but a good technique is first to set it to maximum boost and then sweep through the frequency range to locate the point of interest. After locating the problem area, you can reduce the gain setting to give you the required degree of cut or boost. Adjusting the Q should be done by ear, and in most corrective applications you should use high Q values only for cutting troublesome frequencies and low Qs for gentle boosting.

EXCITERS/ENHANCERS

Also known as enhancers, exciters are devices that add synthesised high-frequency harmonics to a signal in order to make it sound brighter and more detailed. They are used to push sounds to the front of a mix or to create clarity and space in a crowded mix. They're best used sparingly, though, as it's easy to make your material sound harsh by overprocessing it. Enhancers can work well on some vocal sounds, but this kind of overprocessing may exaggerate sibilance. They may also be used to liven up complete mixes, if you have a stereo unit.

THE PROS SAY...

If you find you need lots of EQ on a particular sound, think about the way you recorded it to see if you can get closer to your ideal sound at source.

Home Recording

SUMMARY

There are a great many exciting effects and processors available to us today, but most of the problems I come across when asked to help people with their recordings are due to the excessive or inappropriate use of these devices. A good recording should sound good with no treatment at all, after which appropriate compression (in the case of vocals) and reverb are the most important elements. A useful adage: If in doubt, leave it out!

WEEK 5 TEST

This week's test is geared to discover just how much about the world of EQ and effects has sunk in. Again, if you have any trouble with any of the questions, read the material again until you're comfortable with it.

1 Where would you normally connect an effect?

A In an insert point

B In the effect send/return loop

C In either

2 Where would you normally connect a processor?

A In an insert point

B In the effect send/return loop

C In either

3 If the signal feeding a compressor exceeds the threshold by 10dB but the output level rises by only 2dB, what is the compressor's ratio?

Home Recording

4 Which of these devices are effects and which are processors?

A Reverb

B Echo

C Compression

D Chorus

E Equalisation

5 What type of equaliser has three controls for adjusting gain (cut/boost),

frequency and bandwidth?

WEEK 6

MONITORING

Fact: You can only make good recordings if you have a monitoring system that gives you an accurate impression of what you're recording, and if you want to achieve an adequate level of monitoring accuracy, you need to use appropriate speakers set up in a suitable acoustic environment. The ideal system must be capable of reproducing the entire audio spectrum with the minimum of distortion or colouration, but with the smaller systems used in home studios we have to accept that the very deep bass will never be reproduced entirely accurately because of the limited room size and lack of elaborate acoustic treatment.

 If you install speakers with too much bass extension in a small or inadequately treated room, you'll probably find that some bass notes sound louder than others, which makes judging bass levels a real problem.

For project-studio use, speakers that work down to 45Hz or 50Hz are probably the best compromise, but my advice is to read magazine reviews (check out *Sound On Sound* magazine's website at soundonsound.com, where you can read equipment reviews going back over seven years) before making your choice, as even similarly specified monitor speakers can behave very differently. While carefully chosen hi-fi speakers may be suitable for monitoring use, be aware that many such speakers are designed to flatter the sound rather than represent it as honestly as possible. Speakers specifically designed for monitoring are accurate rather than flattering, and they may also be able to withstand more prolonged use at high listening levels.

Home Recording

ACTIVE OR PASSIVE?

A two-way 'mid-field' monitor with a six- or eight-inch bass/mid speaker usually works best in smaller studios, and active versions (with separate built-in amplifiers for the bass- and high-frequency drivers, fed from a built-in crossover circuit) are often the best choice as they eliminate the guesswork from buying a suitable power amplifier and don't require long runs of speaker cable. If you're unfamiliar with the technology, the larger speaker that handles the bass and mid range is often known as the *woofer* or *bass/mid driver*, while the smaller speaker that handles all the high frequencies is known as the *tweeter* or *HF* (High Frequency) *driver*. The *crossover* is a type of electronic filter that separates the high and low frequencies before feeding them to the two drivers so that each handles only the range of frequencies for which it is designed. This is necessary as it is very difficult to build a single driver that can cover the entire audio spectrum.

In general, active speakers produce better-controlled, tighter-sounding bass than comparable passive models, although there are some good passive speakers around. However, if you choose to use these, don't skimp on the power amplifier as this has a considerable effect on the sound. As a rule, anything less powerful than 75W per channel is probably underpowered for monitoring purposes, as it's essential that signal peaks can be accommodated without distortion. Also, use heavy-gauge speaker cable and observe the polarity of the speaker connections when connecting; in other words, make sure that the red or positive terminal on the power amplifier's speaker output goes to the red terminal on the speaker and that the wires aren't crossed over. You might also want to check that the left and right speakers aren't reversed.

MONITOR POSITION

At mid and high frequencies, the sound of a speaker radiates in a cone from the front, as you'd expect, but as the frequency gets lower, the dispersion pattern widens. Indeed, at very low frequencies, almost as much energy is emitted backwards as forwards. Low-frequency energy reflects from solid walls but tends to pass through less substantial structures, such as doors and lightweight partition walls, and so any solid walls adjacent to and behind the speakers will bounce energy back into the room, making the perceived bass level within the room louder. Designers of monitor speakers take this into account, however, and with active monitors you'll often find switches on the rear panel allowing you to switch between settings depending on whether the speaker is mounted very close to the wall or some distance away from it, thus compensating for the bass rise that occurs close to a solid wall. Passive speakers have no such switches and so are best set up at least several inches away from a solid wall or as the manual guidelines advise.

In order to ensure the smoothest and most accurate bass response, the distances between the speaker and the rear wall should be different from the distance between the speaker and the side walls, and in turn the distance between the speaker and the floor should be different again. The reason for this is simply to randomise these low-frequency bass-boost effects and so minimise the likelihood that some notes will sound much louder than others. If the bass still sounds uneven, try moving the speakers by a few inches to see if you can improve things. Also, make sure that the speakers aren't placed right in the corners of the room, as this results in a very uneven bass response.

Home Recording

In rectangular rooms, it's usually best to set up the speakers along the longest wall, but don't worry too much if this isn't possible. The majority of monitors are intended to be mounted with the tweeter above the bass unit, as this provides the widest listening angle over which the sound is accurate. The tweeters should be positioned at around head height and the speakers should be angled in so that they aim toward the listening position. In other words, when you look at the speakers, the tweeter should be pointing directly at your head. Figure 6.1 shows a good monitoring position.

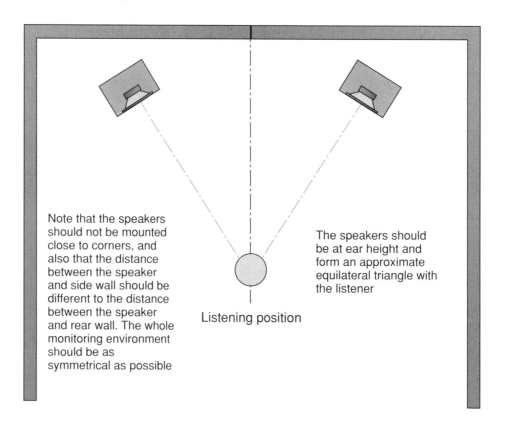

Note that the speakers should not be mounted close to corners, and also that the distance between the speaker and side wall should be different to the distance between the speaker and rear wall. The whole monitoring environment should be as symmetrical as possible

Listening position

The speakers should be at ear height and form an approximate equilateral triangle with the listener

Figure 6.1: Correct monitoring arrangement

Most speakers will sound more accurate if they're positioned on stands a little way behind the mixing console rather than placed on a table, and it's important that the whole setup is symmetrical, with the distance between the speakers being roughly the same as the distance from the listener to each of the speakers.

THE PROS SAY...

Listen to your recording from outside the room. This will tell you a lot more about the balance than sitting right in front of the speakers.

Stands should be solid (some can be filled with sand), with no tendency to vibrate, and the speakers mounted on soft rubber pads, non-slip rubber matting or blobs of picture-mounting goo such as Blu-Tack.

HEADPHONES FOR MONITORING?

Headphones are great problem solvers, as they'll often reveal things that speakers don't, but I wouldn't recommend using them in place of speakers as the bass response and stereo imaging can sound quite different over headphones. On the plus side, headphones are independent of the acoustics of the room in which they are used, and the sense of detail that they convey makes it easier to pick out small noises or distortions that might go unnoticed over speakers. For this reason, it's a good strategy to get a mix sounding right over loudspeakers first, then check for flaws using headphones.

Home Recording

SIMPLE ACOUSTIC TREATMENT

The consequence of using either inaccurate speakers or working in an acoustically difficult room is that your mix might seem fine in your studio but, as soon as it's played back on another system in another room, the tonal balance sounds all wrong, especially at the bass end. Domestic rooms vary considerably in this regard, but one decorated with fitted carpets, soft furnishings and curtains is often quite usable for monitoring using modest-sized speakers. Further improvements can often be made by fixing acoustic foam, quilts or heavy drapes to the walls.

Sound energy emitted by the speakers bounces off every reflective surface in the room, and in order to maximise the accuracy of the monitoring system, the level of reflected sound needs to be kept under control. One way of doing this is by working closer to the speakers (as close as three or four feet) – something known as *near-field monitoring*. Listening to commercial recordings of a similar style to the material you're mixing over your studio system will also help you to gauge the tonal balance of your mix and help you to familiarise yourself with the character of your monitors.

ABSORBERS

You can reduce the amount of reflected sound reaching your listening position by fixing a square metre of acoustic foam tile (ideally four inches thick) to the side wall just in front of your normal listening position and centred at your (seated) head height. To find the exact spot, get someone to hold a mirror on the wall while you sit in your mixing position. When you can see the monitor speaker in the centre of the mixer, that's where you need to fix the centre of your foam tiles. Having the tiles

extend back so they come level with or just behind your listening position will help to kill 'flutter echoes', which can be produced between parallel walls; if you can hear a ringing, resonant echo when you clap your hands, you're hearing a flutter echo.

If you have a low ceiling, it may also help to attach an area of acoustic foam to the ceiling just forward of your listening position. Figure 6.2 over the page shows a practical monitoring layout with sound-absorbing tiles used to dampen out early reflections and flutter echoes, although you may also use heavy drapes or even duvet bedspreads in place of foam if you prefer. Where possible, use three- or four-inch-thick foam tiles – the thicker they are, the more effective they are at lower frequencies. It might also be worth placing some foam on the walls behind the speakers if the front wall is particularly reflective. Note: Figure 6.2 shows a square room, but in practice square or cube-shaped rooms should be avoided.

Some commercial 'acoustics in a box' kits come with triangular foam absorbers designed to even out the low-frequency performance of a room. These shouldn't be needed in rooms that use a dry-wall construction or those that have lots of door and window area, but they might be useful in solidly built rooms with only a small area of window. Triangular bass traps are usually fitted to the front and/or rear corners of a room where the walls meet the ceiling, as this is where they are most effective.

The wall directly behind you will also reflect sound, and in most cases the best strategy for remedying this is simply to break up the reflections by using an uneven surface such as a book case. If the wall is very close to you, fixing a thick acoustic

Acoustic foam on the walls behind the speakers can help to reduce unwanted reflections

Monitor speakers

Potential reflection paths

Listening position

Acoustic foam positioned to prevent reflected sound from the speakers from reaching the listening position. The foam will also help to kill any ringing (flutter echoes) caused by hard, parallel walls

Optional acoustic foam rectangle on ceiling to reduce reflections

Optional foam corner bass traps to reduce unevenness at low frequencies

Fitting shelving to the rear wall will help to break up reflections that would otherwise bounce directly back to the listening area. Soft furnishings, such as a sofa, can also help

Figure 6.2: Acoustic tiles on the side walls and ceiling (showing optional rear bass traps)

foam tile or hanging a duvet directly behind your head can also help.

In a monitoring environment, wall-to-wall carpet is desirable, though not essential, as it helps to kill floor-to-ceiling reflections, while a heavy underfelt will also help with both soundproofing and absorption. However, don't be tempted to carpet the walls or cover large amounts of the room's surfaces in foam as this will soak up all the high frequencies, leaving the room sounding boxy and boomy at low frequencies.

THE PROS SAY...

Don't try to mix a song directly after recording it. Leave it for a few hours or, ideally, for a few days.

Above all, don't confuse acoustic treatment with soundproofing; acoustic treatment is designed to make your listening environment more accurate but often does little or nothing to prevent sound from getting in or out. Soundproofing is largely beyond the scope of this book, but it invariably involves using double-glazed windows and heavy doors with airtight seals all the way around. As a brief introduction to soundproofing, it's enough to know that double doors are more effective than single doors, while walls can only be soundproofed by adding mass (weight) and/or creating a double structure with a gap between which can be stuffed with mineral wool to dampen resonances. Mass can be added to a lightweight wall by fixing multiple layers of plasterboard or gypsum board over the original surface. Unfortunately, there is no lightweight soundproofing solution, and the old myth that egg boxes stuck to the walls somehow control sound leakage is completely without foundation.

Home Recording

Here's the test for this week – a short one this time. If you've read the previous week's material closely, you should have no problem, but if you do come unstuck, read it again until you can answer the questions.

1   Why does the room affect the sound you hear from your speakers?

2   Why is it important that your monitoring system is set up symmetrically?

3   What's the difference between an active and a passive speaker?

WEEK 7

MULTITRACK RECORDING

Multitrack recording was first developed for use with analogue tape, and while analogue tape machines are still in use today (and enjoying a bit of a comeback in some circles), most recording is done using digital media such as digital tape, hard drives, MiniDisc or, in more basic systems, solid-state memory such as SmartMedia. Of the analogue machines still in use by recording musicians, the majority are cassette-based four- or eight-track devices.

It's still easiest to explain the concept of multitracking on an analogue-tape-based system, and in many cases the modern digital counterpart still follows the old analogue paradigm, as far as operation and terminology is concerned. For this reason, it's probably simplest to start by describing the old analogue-tape model.

While a conventional recorder allows you to make a recording of an event in mono or stereo, a multitrack recorder enables musical compositions to be built up in layers that can be recorded and erased independently, which is clearly attractive to solo musicians who want to play and sing many or all of the musical parts themselves. Multitrack recording also allows several different parts to be recorded simultaneously while still being kept separate, which makes it possible to adjust the balance of the different parts after recording. This is the basis of virtually all modern music recording.

Home Recording

TAPE TRACKS

Analogue magnetic tape comprises a flexible strip of plastic coated with a layer of oxide particles designed to retain magnetic information. This tape is drawn at a steady speed across a record head, which imprints the audio signal onto the tape as a varying magnetic charge. An erase head positioned immediately prior to the record head wipes the tape of any previously recorded material before the tape arrives at the record head. When the recording process is finished and the tape machine is set to play, the recorded signal is 'read' either by a separate playback head positioned just after the record head or – as is more often the case in home-studio recorders – by the same head that did the recording. Figure 7.1 shows these head arrangements on both two-head and three-head analogue recorders.

Stereo recorders actually create two different recordings side by side along the tape in the form of two parallel *tracks*. Essentially, the electronics and heads are duplicated, although instead of having two physically separate record heads, there's a single head assembly containing the two heads: one to record the left signal and one to record the right. Similarly, the playback and erase heads follow the two-in-one format (if the playback head is separate from the record head).

MULTITRACK RECORDERS

Multitrack tape machines can typically record from 4 to 24 tracks of audio on 'open-reel' tape – which ranges from a quarter of an inch to two inches in width – or up to eight tracks on analogue compact cassette. An eight-track machine, for example, would have eight sets of record and playback electronics and head assemblies

Figure 7.1: Head arrangements on both two- and three-head analogue recorders

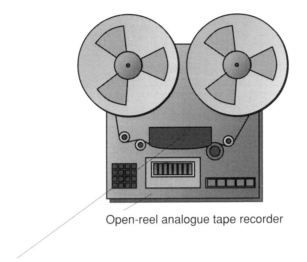

Open-reel analogue tape recorder

Actual position of head assembly

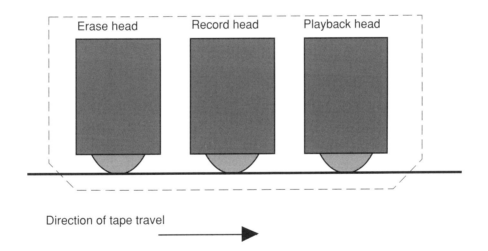

Erase head   Record head   Playback head

Direction of tape travel

containing eight heads, one above the other. Eight tracks is the current maximum for cassette-based systems, with four being more common. Figure 7.2 shows both stereo and eight-track tape formats. Note that, on a multitrack machine, any convenient pair of tracks may be used together to record a stereo signal.

Home Recording

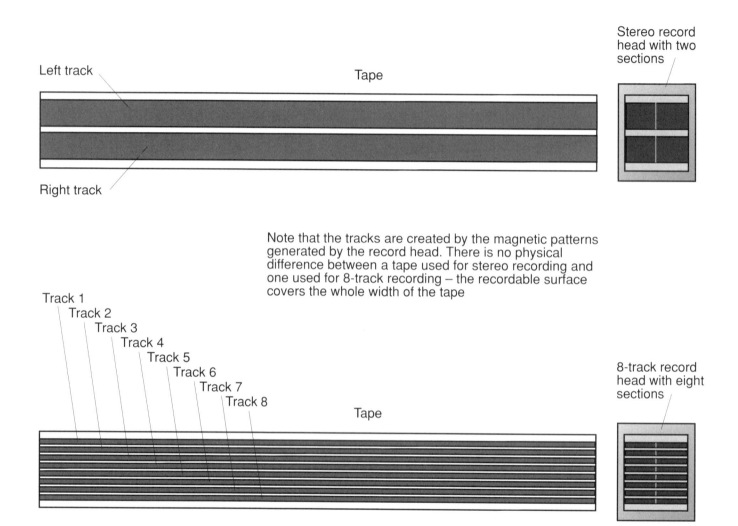

Note that the tracks are created by the magnetic patterns generated by the record head. There is no physical difference between a tape used for stereo recording and one used for 8-track recording – the recordable surface covers the whole width of the tape

Figure 7.2: Stereo (top) and eight-track (bottom) tape formats

The creative power of multitrack recording stems from the fact that these tracks may be recorded all at once, a few at once or just one at a time. Record Ready buttons for the individual tracks determine which tracks go into Record mode when you press Play and Record together. You can either record a live performance in one take, using several microphones, or you can build up your composition on separate

tracks, an instrument at a time. Adding extra instruments and vocals after you've recorded the first part (or parts, if you recorded several tracks at once) is a process known as *overdubbing*.

Using a simple mixer, the levels of the recorded tracks may be balanced in level and panned anywhere between the two speakers to produce an artistically pleasing mix, which is traditionally recorded onto a separate stereo recorder. With suitable hardware (or software, if you use a computer-based recording system), you can also add effects such as echo or reverb as you mix. Some tapeless digital machines also have the facility to record and store their own stereo mixes without the need for an external stereo recorder.

OVERDUBBING

After the first track or tracks have been recorded, the performer needs to have some way of hearing these play back while he or she is overdubbing new parts. An integrated multitracking workstation typically includes a headphone monitoring facility, whereas with a more sophisticated system, comprising a separate mixer and recorder, monitoring would be arranged via the mixer. Without this ability to monitor the recorded signal, you'd have no way of knowing whether or not you were playing the new part in time with the existing tracks. When recording overdubs, monitoring is generally done using headphones to prevent the previously recorded sound from spilling back into the microphone, and fully enclosed headphones work best as they allow very little sound to leak out. When working in the same room as the recorder, any monitor loudspeakers should be switched off while recording is taking place.

Home Recording

As emphasised earlier, a single tape track can be used to record only a mono signal. Stereo signals, such as those sent by the left and right outputs from a stereo drum machine or keyboard, need to be recorded onto two tracks, which must then be panned left and right in the mix to recreate the original stereo image. Modern audio software and some other digital recording systems often provide the choice of selecting either mono or stereo tracks, where a stereo track behaves like two mono tracks operating from a single set of controls. The only significant control difference between mono and stereo tracks is that a mono track has a pan control for stereo positioning while a stereo track has a stereo-balance control to allow you to adjust the left/right balance.

PUNCHING IN AND OUT

Not all of us can record a part for a song all the way through without making a single mistake, so a multitrack recorder needs to allow the user to correct mistakes without starting over from the beginning of the track each time.

The process by which small parts of a recording are replaced with new sections is known as *punching in and out*. On tape machines, punching in and out is simply a way of switching one or more chosen tracks in and out of Record mode without stopping the tape transport. The usual procedure is to put the machine into Play mode with the Record Ready button switched on for only the track you're aiming to fix, and then, just before the faulty part, punch the machine into Record mode (usually by holding down Play while pressing Record), then play or sing over the offending phrase, after which you punch out again. This process allows you to

overwrite short sections of an original recording, and the accuracy with which you can do it depends on your timing with the recorder's transport buttons, as you often need to punch in and out during small gaps between musical phrases or words.

Punching out is most usually achieved by hitting Play, although hitting Stop will also end the recording process. Some recorders also let you use a footswitch for punching in and out, which is very convenient for musicians working on their own.

PUNCH-IN PRACTICALITIES

When overdubbing a new section, you need to hear the existing recording up to the point when you punch in, after which you need to hear the new part you're recording. When you punch out of Record again, the monitoring needs to switch back to playing the recording from tape. Any tracks not armed for recording continue to play normally during a punch-in so you hear the backing parts without interruption. The Auto Monitor mode on the vast majority of recorders does this for you.

When recording music, it helps to make your punch-in and punch-out points coincide with a drum beat, as this helps to hide any slight discontinuities that might occur at the edit points. Analogue tape machines often leave a small gap at the punch-in point, although digital machines are generally seamless in this respect. With instrument parts, it's important to start playing before the punch-in point, as the act of punching in may record over the sustain of a note that was sounding beforehand. By starting playing or singing before the punch-in point, any 'hang over' from sustained notes will be duplicated, making the edit sound more natural.

Home Recording

BOUNCING

If you need to record more parts than you have tracks available, you'll need to learn about a process called *bouncing*. This is where two or more of the already recorded tracks are mixed together and the result is re-recorded (usually in stereo) onto a spare pair of tracks. Bouncing can be done on digital as well as analogue recorders, although computer systems can now support so many audio tracks that bouncing is usually necessary only with entry-level analogue-cassette, solid-state memory and MD-based digital recording workstations, as they seldom offer more than eight tracks. Once you're satisfied that the bounced parts sound OK, you can delete the original tracks and reuse them to add new parts. Of course, this means you can't make any further adjustments to the balance of parts once they've been bounced.

 With analogue tape, there will always be a slight loss of quality whenever you bounce, so make sure you're recording the bounced part at the optimum level. Digital systems lose less quality than analogue during bouncing, although systems with an analogue mixer section will still incur some small degradation.

 While analogue tape can be recorded with the meters occasionally peaking into the red, digital recording systems have no such no safety margin, so when bouncing, as with recording, you have to ensure that your signals are as high as they can be without ever causing the peak or clip indicators on the target tracks to light up.

DIGITAL MULTITRACK

Digital recorders use tracks, just like tape machines, and again it's possible to punch in and out on them, although the exact method of doing so will vary slightly from one machine to another, so always read the manual thoroughly. Computer systems don't always offer manual punching-in or -out facilities, but they invariably include a system whereby you first define the punch-in and -out points and then execute the recording automatically. Moreover, many digital systems allow an unsatisfactory recording to be undone so that you can try again – a very useful feature denied to those who use tape! Digital tape-based systems have essentially the same operational limitations as analogue-tape systems, insomuch as you can only access a recording by winding through the tape until you reach it.

 With analogue tape machines, punching in may leave a small gap at the punch-in point due to the physical distance between the record head and the erase head preceding it. Digital tape and disk-based machines have overcome this limitation, so punching in and out on these devices is generally seamless.

While digital tape machines may be thought of as being very similar to analogue tape machines from an operational point of view, tapeless disk-based systems – which retain the track paradigm, mainly to make the user feel comfortable – are far more flexible. In reality, the audio data recorded to the hard drives of these machines isn't stored in neat, side-by-side rows but in blocks of data, and a process known as random access (a computer term) means that any block of data can be recorded or played at any time, unlike with tape, where you first have to wind through the reel

until you find the section you want. This random-access capability makes possible all kinds of powerful editing capabilities that were quite impossible with tape.

TYPES OF MULTITRACK RECORDING SYSTEM

At their most basic, tape-based multitrack recording systems comprise a multitrack recorder, a mixing console and a separate stereo recorder on which to record the final mixed result. Separate digital recorders are now available that do much the same job as their analogue counterparts, again teamed with an analogue or digital mixer, but the majority of systems used in home recording combine both recorder and mixer in the same unit. The main types available, along with their pros and cons, are listed below.

Separate Components

The original professional recording studio always comprised a separate multitrack tape machine, mixer and master stereo recorder. This arrangement is still possible using digital or analogue multitrack machines, digital or analogue mixers and digital or analogue stereo recorders, in any combination, although this isn't a popular route for the beginner to take due to its cost and complexity. The benefits of using separate systems include the fact that you can connect other pieces of effect or processor hardware relatively easily, and you can upgrade the system in stages. Hard-disk-based digital recorders also tend to include basic copy, move, cut and paste editing facilities, and most have one or more levels of undo.

Cassette Multitrackers

The majority of cassette multitrackers comprise a four- or eight-track recorder paired with a simple mixer for recording and monitoring purposes, although you'll still need a separate stereo recorder to capture the finished mix. Cassette multitrackers are fairly inexpensive and easy to operate, and they use easily available consumer cassette tape. The better ones work at double the speed of domestic cassette recorders to improve the audio quality, and because the whole width of the tape is used to record the four or eight tracks in one direction, the playing time of a C90 cassette tape can be as little as 22 minutes when used on such a machine. Virtually all cassette multitrackers use Dolby or dbx noise reduction to minimise tape hiss, and it's important that this noise reduction is switched on both while recording and replaying in order to get an accurate sound. It's also advisable to use the type of tape recommended by the manufacturer to get the best results.

 Tapes recorded in cassette multitrackers cannot be replayed on domestic stereo cassette players because the tracks are recorded in a different place on the surface of the tape.

Because cassette multitrackers are easy to use, they make good musical notepads for capturing ideas, but their recording quality isn't good enough to make serious release-quality recordings. Furthermore, most have no built-in effects, so if you want to add reverb or echo, you need to connect an external effects box.

Home Recording

! **To cut down on cost, many multitrackers – both analogue and digital – cannot record all of their tracks at once. For example, an eight-track recorder may be able to record only four tracks simultaneously. This isn't a problem if you work by adding a track or two at a time, but it's a serious limitation if you want to record your band live.**

MiniDisc Multitrackers

These are similar in concept to cassette multitrackers but record digital audio data onto a MiniDisc rather than analogue signals onto tape. With tapeless digital recorders, it's possible to design in the ability for the machine to record its own stereo mix, but this is by no means applicable to all models. The audio quality of MD multitrack is subjectively better than audio cassette, and again both four- and eight-track versions are commonplace. As with cassette, the recording time per disc is limited, but the low cost and convenience of the media makes these machines worth considering. Technically speaking, the data compression used in MiniDisc means the audio quality isn't as good as CD, but on most pop material the difference is subtle. Basic editing facilities are also available on most MD multitrack recorders.

You may notice some tapeless digital recorders offering a function termed *virtual tracks*. This is a feature that lets you record several versions of a track, even though you can play only one of these versions back at a time. For example, you might record half a dozen guitar solos onto the virtual tracks of, say, recorder track 8, then decide which one to use later. Virtual tracks take up just as much data storage space as real tracks but are a useful way of extending the capabilities of a system

that has a limited number of 'real' tracks, by which I mean the number of tracks that can be played back simultaneously.

Solid-State Memory

Multitrackers based on Flash memory, such as SmartMedia (the same memory cards as those used in digital cameras), work in much the same way as MiniDisc or hard-disk multitrackers, but they have the advantage that there are no moving parts to wear out and no motors to generate noise. However, the storage media is relatively costly and the recording time they afford can be quite limited.

These machines are small, portable and convenient, with many models allowing recorded data to be backed up onto a computer via USB so that the memory card can be reused. The audio quality they produce depends on the data-compression system used to maximise recording time, and at best they sound as good as MD recorders, with the Long Play modes sounding progressively less hi-fi. This type of machine may also have some built-in effects, such as reverb, and battery-powered pocket-sized recorders are possible using this technology. Some of the models also include a built-in microphone which is of adequate quality for songwriting or recording demos, although their limited facilities and audio quality make them less suitable for serious music production. Basic editing may also be built in.

THE PROS SAY...

Some people never get a chance to consolidate their approach to making music, because what is cutting edge one year is abandoned the next in the constant frenzy to keep up with the latest technology.

Home Recording

Hard-Disk Workstations

Hard-disk multitrackers don't need to compress the data to get enough recording time, although some models do use a subtle form of compression to achieve a high track count. Most of these machines have integral digital mixers with built-in effects and processing, with the digital mixer section invariably utilising multifunction controls to save space. This makes these kinds of multitrackers slightly less intuitive to use than systems that include conventional analogue mixers, but their benefits include good-quality recording, on-board effects and processors and, on most machines, the facility to store mix settings as static 'snapshots' that can be recalled if you need to revisit a song you worked on earlier.

More advanced digital multitrackers may also include dynamic automation (with or without motorised faders), which means that you can record fader, pan and other control movements. (The advantage of mix automation is that you can keep fine-tuning a mix until everything is perfect, after which the mix will play back the same way every time.) It's also quite common for these machines to be able to record a stereo mix without requiring the use of a separate stereo recorder, while more comprehensive models include built-in CD burners, thus enabling the finished tracks to be transferred to a CD-R, which can be played in a domestic CD player; the CD burner may also be used for backing up song data in multitrack form so that it can be remixed later. The usual Cut, Copy and Paste edit modes are also supported, often with more sophisticated editing additions, and top-of-the-line models may also allow you to connect a computer monitor and mouse to provide visual editing features more in keeping with those of a computer-based

DAW (see below). One slight drawback is that some of these machines include cooling fans, which may make some noise, as will the hard drive – something to think about if you wish to record and play in the same room.

Computer DAWs

Computer-based DAWs (Digital Audio Workstations) – comprising a computer, an audio interface, a MIDI interface and suitable music software – have the steepest operational learning curve simply because they can do so much. Not only do they take over the role of the multitrack recorder and mixer, but they also offer effects and processors, mix automation, software instruments and MIDI sequencing. The most

THE PROS SAY...

Back up your work. Many of us have come to learn the hard way: digital data can't be actually considered 'real' unless it exists in at least two different places and ideally in many more.

sophisticated music-software-based systems replicate everything a conventional studio has to offer (except, of course, mics and speakers). On these devices, songs may be mixed entirely within the computer, and finished songs or even complete albums may be burned to CD using the computer's CD-ROM writer.

The graphical interfaces of computer-based DAWs make it easier to rearrange songs after recording and allow MIDI data to be manipulated alongside audio data. (If you're not familiar with MIDI and would like to know more, check out my book *MIDI For The Technophobe*, also published by SMT.) Although it often takes longer to learn how to use software-based systems, they are generally faster to use and are more versatile than their hardware counterparts in terms of editing.

However, be aware that some computers are physically noisy, which again can be a problem if you want to use the same room for both recording and playback.

While hardware-based systems have faders to allow you to control levels, the on-screen fader levels on a computer-based DAW must be adjusted via the mouse, unless you add an optional hardware control surface. Because a mouse can adjust only one fader at a time, mix automation becomes essential rather than a luxury. Hardware surfaces can always be added as your needs become more sophisticated, and in this respect those with motorised faders are the most intuitive to use.

MORE ABOUT RANDOM ACCESS

The main editing strength of computer systems and, to a lesser extent, most hardware digital workstations is that of random-access editing – the ability to access data instantaneously (almost!) anywhere on a hard drive or some other form of tapeless storage medium. Random access allows you to rearrange your music in much the same way as you might use a word processor to edit a document. In practical terms, this means you're able to use on-screen tools to cut, copy, move or delete sections of audio in an arrangement, usually without actually changing the original recorded data in any way. For example, if you copy a chorus to a new location in the song, what you hear on playback is the originally recorded chorus; the hard drive simply locates it and plays it back as required. You can also offset the timing of one audio track against another, something that's impossible on a tape-based system.

Using the editing capabilities of a typical software system, you can copy one good vocal chorus part to all your choruses, or you can record several versions of a vocal and then comp(ile) a new vocal part using the best words and phrases from the various takes. You can also duplicate entire verses or completely rearrange a song without affecting the original recorded data. This capacity for creative editing is almost limitless and is something tape users can only dream about.

MIXING

As I said earlier, the art of mixing was originally called balancing, because the main part of the job was to adjust the relative balance of all the voices and instruments that made up a song. If the tracks have been recorded carefully, it should be possible to set up a reasonable initial balance without resorting to EQ or other processing.

When it comes to mixing pop music, I like to work on the drum and bass balance first, but I'm always aware that the apparent balance will change when the rest of the instruments and voices are added. It's only when all the instruments are in place that you should concern yourself with the finer points of EQ and balance as mixed tracks can sound very different when heard in isolation.

TOP TIP

If the recording includes vocals, try to set these at a level that sits comfortably in the mix. If the vocals are too quiet, you won't hear the lyrics clearly, but if they're too loud, they won't sound like part of the overall performance.

Home Recording

Once a reasonable balance has been achieved, you can add effects and work on the stereo positioning of the different sounds. The most important effect is probably vocal reverb, but don't overdo it – just use enough to get the vocal to sit comfortably in the mix. A plate reverb setting with a 1.6–2.2-second decay time works well, and adding 60–80ms of pre-delay can make the sound bigger and richer. If you need to use EQ, be aware that cutting frequencies you don't want generally sounds more natural than boosting frequencies you want to hear more of unless you're very subtle.

TOP TIP

Bass drums, bass guitars, bass synths and other low-frequency sounds are invariably panned to the centre as this helps to spread the load of these high-energy frequencies between both speakers. Usually, lead vocals are also positioned centrally, for artistic reasons.

Backing vocals and other instruments can be panned to one side or split and panned left and right if there's more than one part. However, it's usefully desirable to maintain a sense of symmetry, so if there's a guitar on one side it might work well to balance it with a keyboard on the other.

TOP TIP

It can be very helpful to listen to the balance of your mix in progress from outside the room with the door left open. If anything is too loud, or if the vocals are getting lost, this test will tell you immediately. Also, check out rough mixes on as many different systems as possible, including your car's sound system.

CHANGES WHILE MIXING

Once you've got an initial balance, you'll probably need to make a few further small adjustments during the mix, especially if you have instruments that need to be turned up during solos. Adding a little compression to vocals will help to keep them at an even level, but further adjustment may be needed even so, depending on the singer's skill in controlling their dynamics. Where necessary, you can 'ride' the vocal fader during the mix to bring the level up slightly whenever the vocals become lost or to pull it back when they're too loud.

Mix automation makes it easy to fine-tune the mix balance a track at a time, but on a manual mix the various level settings and changes should be marked clearly on the console with wax pencil so that you know exactly how far to move the faders. Use the time counter to mark exactly when to make the adjustments.

Gates or expanders can be helpful in cleaning up tracks that include a steady level of background noise, although care must be taken here to match the release time

of the gate to the sound being processed so that the natural decay of the sound isn't cut short. You can also use gates or manual mutes to silence tracks that aren't playing, such as the main vocals during instrumental solos or the solo electric guitar on each side of a solo break. Back in the old days, mixer faders would be pulled right down (or muted) when no part was playing on that track so as not to contribute background noise to the mix, and this is something you can do very easily if you have mix automation. Computer users can also create cleaner mixes by silencing all unwanted sections of a track using their sequencer's muting facilities. For serious mixes, check every track in isolation prior to mixing and eliminate any coughs, clunks or guitar hum before you start mixing.

THAT 'PRODUCED' SOUND

Even if you're using relatively basic equipment, you can still achieve a highly produced sound through the careful use of effects and processors in conjunction with good recording practices. Even drums don't have to be a problem, as today there are some great drum samples and sample loops to work from, and if you want a 'played' drum feel but don't have the facilities to mic up a complete drum kit, there are some excellent electronic drums or drum pads available for triggering samples.

A polished, produced sound starts with a good musical arrangement where the performance is in time, is in tune and uses suitably chosen sounds. The main goal is to have your lead vocal sitting nicely with the backing track so that it sounds part of the same performance and not like it's been stuck on afterwards.

Poorly recorded guitars and basses are a dead giveaway, and no amount of EQ will fix a bad sound. If you can't mic an amp for whatever reason, use a recording preamp designed for guitars as these make light work of getting a good sound (often in stereo) without spill. The same unit will also probably give good results on bass guitar, with a little tweaking.

TOP TIP

If the arrangement features two guitars, try to use two different guitar sounds so that the parts don't blur into one. If the sound is still too busy, think about simplifying one of the parts and re-recording it or using one distorted guitar part in combination with a relatively clean guitar part.

Also consider using different chord inversions for one of the guitar parts, and if you want something cleaner and more organic-sounding, try using an acoustic guitar in place of an electric guitar for rhythm parts.

It's safest to EQ the bass when the rest of the track is playing – it might sound great on its own but then get completely lost when you pull up the other faders. A bass can often be made to sit better in the track by boosting it at around 250Hz to emphasise its woody, mid-range tonality.

Home Recording

Take care when choosing synth sounds as many factory patches sound wonderful in isolation but take up too much space in a mix. Either edit the patches or try using EQ to tame excess bass or high end.

Whatever sounds you choose, it's usually best not to let your arrangements get too busy, as a certain degree of space can be just as important in a mix as the music. Listen to some good commercial records before and during your mixing session – you may be surprised at how few parts are playing at any one time.

It's not only instruments that fill up space; using too much reverb can have the same effect. Short and bright reverbs are less damaging in this respect than long, dark settings, and other effects should also be used carefully. You should only use an effect if the track needs it, not because you've just bought it!

BASS IN THE MIX

When adjusting bass sounds, you need to appreciate that not everyone has large studio monitors at home. Your mix needs to sound good on all kinds of systems, from small domestic hi-fis to full-range club PA systems. This might mean compromising to some extent, but it's important to choose bass sounds that are audible on smaller systems rather than rely on big speakers designed literally to shake your audience. For example, boosting down at 40Hz may sound great on a club PA system, but it's almost an octave below what most small sound systems can reproduce, so you need to ensure that there's also enough energy in the 70–120Hz range.

TOP TIP

Bass sounds often come across as being warmer and more solid if you add

mild distortion using a guitar pedal, a tube processor or a suitable software

plug-in.

A FINAL THOUGHT

Musical production isn't something you add like paint at the end of the recording

process; it's the result of attention to detail at all points throughout the

recording and mixing processes. It starts with the musical arrangement, the

choice of sounds...and of course, a great performance. The main tool you have

isn't the latest effects box or mic preamp but your ears, so use them!

The final point I'd like to make here is that a well-played, well-arranged, well-

recorded piece of music is usually very easy to mix. If the recording falls below

scratch in any of these areas, the mix engineer's job will be very much harder.

Home Recording

After the previous week's study, here are a few

questions to make sure you really do know what you

think you know!

1 Which type of recording system allows random-access editing?

A Tape recorder

B Hard-disk-based digital recorder

2 Which pan positions are best for lead vocals?

4 Which pan positions are best for lead kick drums and bass?

5 What's a simple way of checking that your mix sounds balanced?

WEEK 8

SETTING UP A HOME STUDIO

In a commercial recording studio, the nerve centre of the studio is the mixing console, but if you have a cassette multitracker, MiniDisc recorder or hard-disk-based multitrack workstation, the mixer and multitrack recorder are integrated into a single piece of hardware. This reduces space and the amount of wiring required to make the whole system operational, and also makes it more portable.

Computer-based systems also include mixing facilities on their internal tracks and other sounds, but a hardware mixer is still necessary if you have hardware MIDI instruments that you want to add to the mix. Furthermore, a hardware mixer provides a convenient means of adjusting your studio monitor levels and of switching CD players and stereo recorders into the system.

OTHER HARDWARE

Although it's possible simply to plug a microphone or two into your multitracker, put on a pair of headphones and start recording, unless you're going to work at a very basic level you're going to need some other hardware to go with it. If you have a computer system or integrated workstation that includes a CD burner, you probably don't need a separate stereo recorder, but if your system is based around tape or is a type of digital recorder that can't also record its own stereo mix, you'll need a stereo recorder of some kind. For high-quality demos or small-scale releases, a stereo MD recorder is a good choice, as is a CD recorder. If you're planning on releasing the music commercially, however, it may be best to store the mix as a 24-bit audio data file (typically WAV or AIFF) rather than as an audio file, as

Home Recording

this format gives the mastering engineer the most flexibility and reduces the risk of data errors occurring on the audio CD recordings.

THE MONITORING SYSTEM

For serious monitoring, you also need either a pair of passive monitor speakers and a suitable stereo amplifier or a pair of active studio monitors. If you're going to use your hi-fi for monitoring as well as for playing records and CDs, make sure that your hi-fi amplifier has an aux, CD or tuner input spare – you can plug your multitracker's stereo monitor output into any of these. Don't use the phono inputs, though, as these have built-in tonal-correction facilities designed specifically for record decks. Headphones are great quality-control tools and they allow you to carry on working at antisocial hours, so always budget for at least one set of phones, while you might also need to spring for other sets for the performers.

THE PROS SAY...

Getting a good vocal sound using a Mac or PC is no easier or more difficult than if you're using digital tape or an analogue open-reel recorder.

HEADPHONE TYPES

Although mixing entirely on headphones is not recommended, they are essential for monitoring performers while overdubbing. If you're looking to avoid sound leakage, the fully enclosed type that sits over the ears is best. For checking mixes, it doesn't matter whether you buy fully enclosed or semi-open phones, but try to get the most honest-sounding phones you can rather than those designed to flatter.

If multiple performers need to wear headphones at the same time, you'll need to buy a small headphone distribution amplifier with multiple outputs and individual level controls. You can feed the headphone distribution amplifier from your system's headphone output or from the pre-fade send on a mixer or workstation.

MICROPHONES

You'll need at least one decent microphone to record vocals and acoustic instruments, and depending on how you record, you might need more than one, especially if two or more performers are to be recorded at the same time. Unidirectional (cardioid-pattern) capacitor mics are usually the best option for vocals and acoustic instruments, although in order to use them you'll need a mixer that can supply phantom power. Not all integrated multitrackers have phantom power, in which case a battery-powered back-electret capacitor mic might be the best solution. You'll also need pop shields and mic stands.

EFFECTS

If your computer or workstation has built-in effects, this makes life a lot easier, but if not there are many inexpensive multi-effects boxes that give great results. The most useful effect is the reverb processor, but most of today's effect units provide a whole range of different effects in addition to reverb. Often these units allow you to combine several effects and use them simultaneously, but you'll still need one good reverb unit as a minimum requirement. The ideal solution is to have one good reverb unit and one general-purpose multi-effects unit.

Home Recording

PATCHBAYS

In a system where connections need to be changed regularly, a patchbay (sometimes called a 'patch panel') can help to simplify things. For example, you may have a compressor that needs to be patched into different mixer insert points as required, or you may want to move an effect unit from one send to another.

Essentially, a patchbay is a panel with two rows of jack sockets at the front, where the bottom-row sockets are designated inputs and the top row are outputs, and any line input or output connections on your equipment can be connected to the rear of the patchbay using screened cables. The advantage here is that you can then connect any input to any output using short patch cables plugged into the front of the panel. Without the patchbay, you'd have to go around the back of your mixer and effect units and reroute long lengths of cable.

However, it rarely makes sense to bring absolutely everything out to a patchbay, because there are some things you may never need to change, so don't make your patching system any more complicated than it needs to be. Often you'll need patchbay access only for things like recorder line inputs, mixer insert points and mixer sends and returns, plus the inputs and outputs of your effects and processors. Plan your needs before setting up a patchbay, and use adhesive labels to tell you what all the sockets are connected to!

The most common form of jack patchbay uses standard jacks both for patching and for rear-panel connections, which means you can wire up your entire system using

conventional jack leads, making it easy to reconfigure your patchbay when you want to integrate a new piece of equipment. You can now buy patchbays that accommodate both balanced and unbalanced jacks, although a balanced-type bay can handle both balanced and unbalanced signals, so it's the most flexible choice.

The most common type of jack patchbay fits a 1U, 19-inch rack panel and has two rows of 24 sockets, one above the other. A similar number of sockets at the rear is used to connect the patchbay to the various pieces of studio equipment via permanent cables, although if you enjoy soldering you can buy models with 'hard-wired' rear connections so you don't have to keep forking out for jack plugs.

PATCHING CONNECTIONS

Where a patchbay is used to provide access to the ins and outs of effects and processors, to the input channels of a mixer, or to the mixer's send and return jacks, etc, the socket at the back of the patchbay connects directly to the socket on the front and nowhere else. Such a connection system is described as being *non-normalised*. You can think of the sockets on the front panel as being simply extensions of whatever the patchbay is connected to, so you need to plug in a cable to make a connection.

NORMALISING

When it comes to insert points, a different type of patchbay is needed where the upper and lower sockets are connected by means of so-called *normalising contacts* when no patch cable plugs are inserted. With this kind of system, the

Home Recording

signal flow remains unbroken until patch cables are inserted to divert the signal flow through an external device. Good patchbays should also come with connection details explaining how to set up normalised and non-normalised connections. For full details on how patchbays are connected, see my book *Home Recording Made Easy* (second edition, also published by SMT), which covers all of the topics in this book in much greater depth but without getting over-technical.

THE SYSTEM

Figure 8.1 shows a home recording system based around an integrated multitracker. All cables should be kept as short as possible and proper screened cabling should be used for all signal connections. Here a domestic hi-fi amp is used for monitoring, which gives you the advantage of being able to mix to your hi-fi's cassette or MiniDisc recorder, if it has one. If your multitracker has a built-in CD burner, this may be used to store CD-quality mixes.

Try to set up your equipment so that everything is within reach and the speakers are positioned symmetrically about the listening position. Most integrated multitrackers are small enough to be set up on a small shelf above a keyboard, if that's your main instrument, and because they tend not to be too noisy, they're usually suitable for recording vocals or acoustic guitars in the same room.

In order to connect external effects boxes, you'll need a multitrack workstation or a separate mixer fitted with effects send and return facilities, and all but the very cheapest musical-notepad-type multitrackers have aux sends and returns for this

Hi-fi power amplifier
(If the multitracker has no built-in CD recorder, a
stereo recorder may be connected to the tape in
and out sockets of the amplifier)

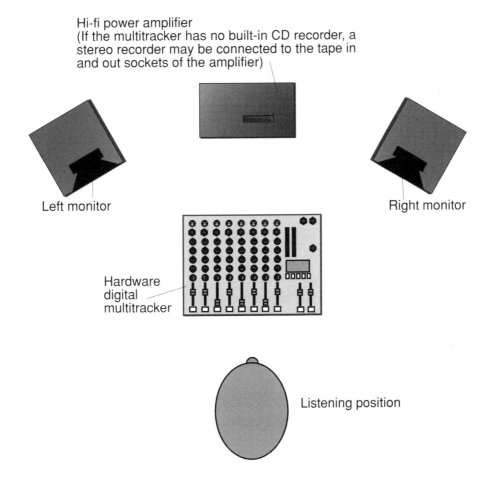

Left monitor

Right monitor

Hardware
digital
multitracker

Listening position

**Figure 8.1: Workstation recording system
with other studio components**

purpose. As I explained earlier, digital effect units have stereo outputs, so at

least one stereo aux return or a couple of spare input channels is required.

Always set the Mix control of an effects device connected via the effects

send/return loop to 100% effect.

![CRASH COURSE]

Home Recording

Figure 8.2 shows a simple system based around a computer and soundcard plus a small mixer. (Refer to Figure 4.4 from Week 4, 'Mixers', to see how the mixer is connected to allow recording and monitoring at the same time.) The mixer's main outputs feed the two soundcard inputs, enabling up to two different parts (either single signals or mixes of signals) to be recorded simultaneously. As with the basic multitracker setup, the soundcard outs feed the mixer's two-track In sockets and

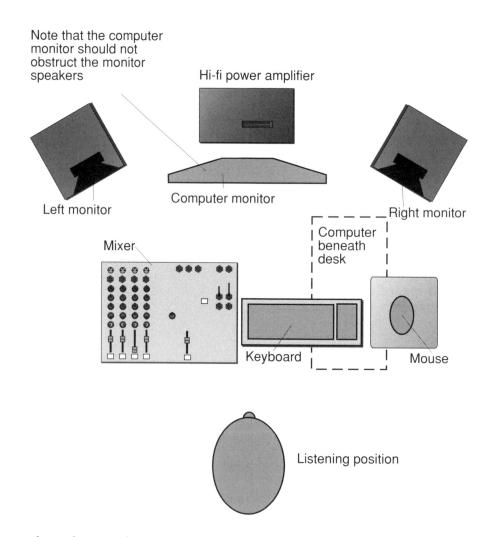

Figure 8.2: System based around a computer and soundcard plus a small mixer

the monitor selector is set to '2-track' so that the control-room monitor-level control affects the level sent to your speakers without interfering with what's being recorded. If you use MIDI with such a system, you'll need to add a basic MIDI interface (or use a keyboard with MIDI USB support), and this simple arrangement assumes that you use only software instruments.

THE PROS SAY...

Surround sound? Very few people seem to have surround speakers connected to their DVD systems and most of those who do use the hideous speakers that come with their TV set.

You can set up a slightly more elaborate system – still based around a two-in/two-out soundcard – by adding a couple of external synth modules and a MIDI interface. In such a system, the mixer may be used conventionally to combine the soundcard outputs with the outputs from your MIDI sound modules, while a separate voice channel or mic preamp can be used for recording directly to the soundcard. However, if you want to record only one audio track at once, you can still use one of the mixer channels (with the fader turned down) and then send the signal to the soundcard input from the mixer's pre-fade send output jack, as described in Week 4. The channel's pre-fade send control sets the recording level.

The mixed signal may then be recorded to an external stereo recorder, although many users prefer to patch the output of the mixer back into the inputs of their soundcard when mixing so that the complete mix can be recorded back into the computer as a new stereo track. The stereo audio file thus created may then be burned to an audio CD-R disc via the computer's own CD burner.

Home Recording

ESSENTIAL EFFECTS AND PROCESSORS

The most important signal processor is the compressor, which helps to keep your levels under control. Signal processors are connected via mixer insert points, so once again, if your system doesn't have integrated compressors, make sure that your hardware has channel insert points so you can connect one. If you don't have insert points, you might be better off buying a combined mic preamp and compressor (voice channel) so that you can compress the vocals and instruments as you record. If you compress the signal before feeding it into a digital recorder, this will also help to prevent accidental overloads.

 You can't plug a microphone directly into a compressor (or any other signal processor, for that matter) designed for line-level use because the signal from the mic is far to low in level.

Where the recording system is computer-based and the host software supports audio plug-ins, you can use software compressors and other processors along with various effects, such as reverb and echo. Software mixers tend to be organised along similar lines as traditional analogue mixers, complete with insert points and aux sends and returns, although each system is slightly different. Instead of using patch cables, the available plug-ins are usually shown via a menu when you click on an insert point or aux send/return loop slot. As a rule, where the channel being processed is stereo, a stereo version of the plug-in will be selected automatically.

Home Recording

A huge advantage of working with plug-ins is that all of your settings are saved along with your song data. The disadvantage is that more plug-ins equals a proportional drain on computer power, and at some point the system will be fully loaded. With a modern machine, this is rarely an issue, although some high-quality reverb and software instrument plug-ins impose heavy demands on computing power.

MUSICAL CONNECTIONS

Home studios are usually wired up via instrument-type jack leads or RCA phono hi-fi cables. Professional microphones require XLR three-pin cables, although some budget multitrackers are designed to accept their mic inputs on balanced jack plugs, and the more serious models will have balanced XLR mic inputs and possibly phantom-power capability. Multitrack workstations and cassette decks usually connect to the hi-fi power amplifier by means of standard RCA phono leads. In more advanced systems, the connections between recorders or audio interfaces and mixers may be balanced, in which case balanced (TRS) jack cables should be used to minimise hum and interference.

Passive speakers should be connected using heavy twin cable, while active speakers are generally connected using balanced XLR mic cables or balanced TRS jack cables.

Setting up a system using a separate mixer and multitrack recorder requires multiple cables to carry the mixer's group outputs to the multitrack machine's inputs and to link the multitrack recorder's output to the mixer's inputs. All signal cables

must be screened, and where multiple cables are required, a multicore cable may be a tidier solution than individual cables. The wiring of this type of system is beyond the immediate scope of this book, as mixers designed specifically for multitracking use are more sophisticated than the basic mixers explained here.

MAINS WIRING

Mains-power wiring should be kept as far away from the signal wiring as possible. Where the cables must cross, it's best if they do so at right angles in order to reduce the amount of interference picked up from the 50Hz or 60Hz mains supply. Avoid having signal cables and mains cables running side by side, as the signal cable may pick up hum radiated by the mains cable.

SAFETY

- **Don't remove the ground leads from any equipment that's supposed to be grounded.**

- **Check mains plugs regularly. Not only are loose wires dangerous but they will also cause intermittent crackles and buzzes.**

ERGONOMICS

In the larger studio, it may not be possible to reach everything from one position, so at least try to arrange things so that you can easily access the controls you use most often. It's also important that you're sitting in the correct position relative to your monitor loudspeakers when you're mixing or adjusting equipment that affects

the sound. If you play keyboards, you may be able to set up to one side of the mixing position, or even arrange a sliding stand beneath the mixer, if there's room.

While it's quite common to see speakers standing on a shelf, on a table or on top of a mixing console, they invariably sound better on stands behind your equipment desk or mixer, as this cuts down on unwanted reflections from the desk. The optimum listening position – sometimes called the *sweet spot* – is exactly between the speakers. In order to ensure that the sweet spot is as wide as possible, the speakers should be angled so that the tweeters are at head height and point either at or just behind the listener's head.

ACOUSTICS

You shouldn't need to do much to a domestic room to make it suitable for mixing good-quality demos or even mixes intended for independent CD release, but it's worth revisiting Week 6, 'Monitoring', to see what inexpensive improvements you can make. In most cases, placing absorbers (quilts, foam or heavy curtains) on either side of the listening position, or possibly behind the speakers, can help, as can breaking up rear-wall reflections by fixing shelves there. It may also be advantageous to place an absorber on the ceiling above your mixing position, extending to a height above the mixer, in order to cut down reflections from that source. However, as a home studio will never be as accurate as a properly designed commercial facility, it's essential that you listen to commercial recordings via your monitoring system to help you get accustomed to how your mixes should sound.

Home Recording

SUMMARY

The most important aspect of making a good recording is in getting a good performance in an acoustically suitable space, closely followed by taking care to place the microphones in the best position to capture the sound you want. In my experience, most recording problems are caused by not enough attention being paid to capturing the best possible sound at source and then trying to rescue the situation with EQ and signal processing. Even the best engineer struggles when faced with a poor recording, so if you concentrate on the essentials, improvising acoustic treatment where necessary, you should be able to make great recordings.

THE PROS SAY...

One of my dreams is to have computer error messages that actually tell you what's wrong rather than simply saying 'An error type −6042 has occurred'.

Many of the classic pop records of the 1950s were made using mixers with no EQ and just mono or stereo recorders. Everything had to be got right at source, including the balance, but when you *do* get it right, it sounds great and you need very little in the way of effects to add the final polish. If you can master the essentials of putting a microphone in the right place to capture the sound you want, you'll have mastered the most important skill in recording music.

WEEK 8 TEST

This is it – your final test for this course! You should be able, by now, to answer the questions listed below, but if not, the same rule applies: no fails, just have another read-through until you can. Good luck!

1   If you were connecting a mixer insert point to a patchbay, should the patchbay sockets be normalised or non-normalised?

2   Why is it less than ideal to stand monitor speakers on a desk or table?

3   What type of cable should you use to connect passive loudspeakers?

4   Why is accurate monitoring important?

GLOSSARY

Audio

Area of technology related to sound recording, processing, amplification and reproduction.

AC

Abbreviation of *alternating current*, a dynamic electrical signal that changes regularly from positive to negative polarity. Audio signals are an example of alternating current, although the term more normally applies to mains electricity power supplies operating at a fixed frequency.

AES/EBU

Digital interfacing standard for transferring stereo audio data from one system or another. The connection standard is a balanced XLR, and regular mic cables may be used for short-distance communication, although specialised digital cable is recommended.

Active

Describes a circuit containing components that can amplify, such as valves, ICs, transistors or FETs. The opposite of *passive*. Loudspeaker systems with built-in amplifiers and crossovers are said to be active.

A-To-D Converter

Abbreviation of *analogue-to-digital converter*, a device for converting analogue signals to a stream of digital numbers. The signal is sampled at regular intervals and the instantaneous level is represented as a binary number.

Ambience

Perceived effect of the environment on a sound due to sound reflections and absorption from surfaces. Heavily reflective environments are said to be reverberant.

Amplify

To increase the amplitude (magnitude) of an electrical signal.

Amplitude

Level or magnitude of an electrical signal, expressed in volts.

Analogue

Describes a continuously changing electrical signal (unlike digital signals, which comprise a series of steps).

Anechoic

Describes an acoustic environment designed to absorb virtually all sound so as to produce no significant reflections.

Attenuate

To reduce the level of an electrical signal.

Aux Send

Mix-buss output designed specifically for driving external effects or foldback systems. (See *Pre-Fade* and *Post-Fade*.)

Axis

Imaginary line depicting the primary direction of transmission or reception of an audio transducer such as a microphone or loudspeaker.

Backup

Safety copy of a tape, digital audio data or software.

Balance

Ratio existing between the left and right channels in a stereo system.

Balanced Wiring

Cabling system using two out-of-phase conductors within a common screen. When balanced equipment is connected onto both ends of the cable, any interference affecting the cable is cancelled out, resulting in a cleaner signal, especially when using longer cables. Most microphones used in recording are balanced.

Band

Specific range of frequencies. In audio, this usually means a section of the audio spectrum.

Bandwidth

Range of frequencies that are passed by an electronic circuit.

Boost/Cut Control

Control which allows a range of frequencies to be either increased or decreased in level. In the centre position, the control has no effect.

Binary

Describes a numbering system comprising ones and zeros. Binary mathematics is the basis of virtually all computer operations.

Bit

Abbreviation of the term *binary digit* describing the smallest piece of binary information, which may be either a one or a zero.

Bouncing

Process of mixing two or more tracks from a multitrack recorder and simultaneously recording the result back to another track.

Buffer

Section of computer RAM used for the temporary storage of data. Also refers to an analogue circuit designed to reinforce a signal without changing its level.

Bus(s)

Electrical signal path onto which other signals may be mixed – for example, a mixer uses a mix buss to combine the various channel signals. Different mixer busses are used to carry the stereo mix, the aux sends and so on. The term *buss* is also applied to power cables that supply numerous destinations – for example, to the individual circuit boards inside a mixer.

Byte

Piece of digital data comprising eight bits.

Cannon Connector

Proprietary brand of XLR connector.

Capacitor

Electronic component comprising two spaced conductors

Home Recording

coupled electrostatically. The space between the conductors may be air or some other non-conducting dielectric material.

Capacitor Microphone

Professional recording microphone that works operates via changes in electrical capacitance. Capacitor mics require phantom power to operate, usually 48V.

Cardioid

Describes a type of microphone pickup pattern exhibited by a mic that picks up sounds from mainly one direction. These mics may also be known as *unidirectional*.

Channel

Input signal path of a mixer and its associated controls.

Chorus

Effect using delay and pitch modulation to create the audio effect of two or more musicians playing the same part.

Clipping

Type of distortion where the top of a waveform is truncated above a certain threshold. Usually occurs when a circuit is forced to handle a higher-level signal than it was designed to.

Clock

Electronic circuit designed to generate precisely spaced pulses for timing applications such as analogue-to-digital conversion, or to drive a digital processor.

Clone

Exact copy. In digital recording, the term relates to a digital transfer of a tape or disk where the data is exactly identical to the original material.

Compressor

Processor designed to reduce the dynamic range of an audio signal.

Conductor

Material that presents little resistance to the flow of electrical current.

Crossover

Electrical circuit designed to separate high and low frequencies prior to feeding loudspeakers.

Cutoff Frequency

Frequencies at which the gain of an amp or filter falls by 3dB.

Cut And Paste

Editing term that originated with word-processing applications. It describes the process of copying or moving data from one place to another.

D-To-A Converter

Abbreviation of *digital-to-analogue converter*, a circuit designed to convert a digitised signal back into an analogue signal. Also known as a DAC.

Daisy Chain

To connect two or more devices in series (so that the

output of one device feeds the input of the next device along, and so on).

DAT

Abbreviation of *digital audio tape*, used with DAT recorders.

Data

Information stored in digital (usually binary) form.

dB

Short for *decibel*, used to express the relative levels of pairs of electrical voltages, powers or sounds.

dBm

Reference level where 0dBm = 1mW into 600 ohms.

dBv/dBu

Reference level where 0dBv (or 0dBu) = 0.775V.

dBV

Reference level where 0dBV = 1V.

dB Per Octave

Measure of the slope of a filter circuit.

DC

Abbreviation of *direct current*.

Decay

Time it takes for a reverberatory or echoing sound to fall in level by 60dB. Also used to describe the closing of an envelope-generating circuit.

Desk

Alternative word for mixer or console.

Depth

Amount by which one parameter is modulated by another – for example, vibrato or chorus depth.

Detent

Mechanical click-stop designed to indicate the centre of the range a rotary control such as a pan pot or EQ cut/boost control.

Dielectric

Describes an insulating layer between the two conductors of a capacitor.

Digital Audio

Describes an electronic device that works by representing electrical signals as a series of binary numbers.

Digital Delay

Digital processor for generating delay or echo effects.

Digital Reverb

Digital processor for recreating reverberation.

DIN Connector

Type of multipin connector with several possible pin configurations. MIDI uses a five-pin, 180° DIN plug and socket.

Disc

Media such as CD or MiniDisc. Excludes computer floppy

Home Recording

and hard disks, which end with the letter k to signify that they are abbreviations of the word *diskette*.

Distortion

Any measurable difference (other than in amplitude) between an input signal and an output signal.

Double Tracking

Process of recording the same performance twice onto two different tape tracks. When the two parts are played back, the effect of two people playing or singing together is created. Double tracking is often employed to thicken up the sound of weak vocals.

Driver

Term applied to the mechanical part of a loudspeaker. Also refers to a piece of software that enables a hardware peripheral or internal card to interface with a computer.

Dry Signal

Sound source which has no added effect. Conversely, a sound treated with an effect, such as reverberation or echo, is often referred to as being *wet*.

Dynamic Microphone

Microphone that uses a moving coil in a magnetic field to generate an output signal.

Dynamic Range

Range between the highest and lowest levels of a signal, usually expressed in decibels.

Echo

Effect created by repeating the original signal, often several times, after a short time delay.

Edit

To change recorded data or data stored on a computer in some way.

Effect

Device designed to add special effects to a sound. Examples include delay, reverb, pitch shifting, chorus, flanging, ADT, phasing and vibrato.

Effect Send

Mixer output designed specifically to feed an external effects unit.

Effect Return

Additional mixer input used to feed an effect unit back into a mix.

Electret Microphone

Type of microphone based on a permanently charged capacitor capsule.

Envelope

Overall amplitude contour of an electrical waveform.

Erase

To remove data from a recording system and replace it with silence. Recordings may also be erased by recording new material in place of the original material.

Equaliser

Device used to increase or decrease selectively the level of specific parts of the audio spectrum relative to others.

Fader

Slider-type control, as opposed to a rotary control.

Filter

Circuit that amplifies or attenuates a band of frequencies.

Flanging

Delay effect using modulation and feedback to produce a sweeping sound.

Foldback

Also known as *cue*, a system for providing performers with a separate mix which they can listen to while recording or overdubbing.

Format

Process applied to a computer disk before it can be used to store data. Formatting effectively creates 'compartments' into which data can be stored.

Frequency

Number of cycles of a repetitive waveform that occur each second.

Frequency Response

Measurement of the frequency range that can be accurately handled by a piece of electrical equipment, microphone or loudspeaker.

FX

Slang term for 'effects'.

Gain

Amount by which a signal is amplified.

Gate

Device designed to shut off a signal when it falls below a specific threshold level.

Glitch

Unwanted pop or click that gets recorded onto tape. These inconsistencies are often due to electrical interference from an outside source.

Graphic Equaliser

Equaliser that uses several faders to provide cut or boost over a narrow range of frequencies.

Ground

Electrical connection to earth.

Ground Loop

Wiring problem where multiple ground paths result in unwanted hum being added to an audio signal.

Hard-Disk Recording

Process of recording digitised audio onto a hard disk rather than onto tape.

HF

Abbreviation of *high frequency*.

Home Recording

High-Pass Filter

Filter that passes signals above a specified frequency and attenuates those falling below that frequency.

Impedance

The 'AC resistance' of a circuit.

Inductor

Electrical component – usually some form of coil – that exhibits inductance. Inductors have a higher impedance at high frequencies than they have at low frequencies.

Insulator

Material with very high resistance that effectively prevents an electric current from flowing.

Insert Point

Connection socket allowing an external processor to be inserted in series with a signal.

Interface

Device that converts one form of data or signal to another – for example, a MIDI interface allows MIDI information to be generated and read by a computer.

I/O

Abbreviation of *input/output*.

Jack Plug

Common semi-professional recording and instrument audio connector. Jack plugs may be either mono or stereo.

Jack Socket

Receptacle for jack plug.

Keyboard

Musical interface based on the piano keyboard but electrical in operation. Also refers to a computer keyboard based on the QWERTY typewriter.

kHz

Magnitude of 1,000Hz (1,000 cycles of a waveform per second).

LCD

Abbreviation of *liquid-crystal display*.

LED

Abbreviation of *light-emitting diode*, a solid-state lamp.

LFO

Abbreviation of *low-frequency oscillator*, used as a source of modulation.

Limiter

Device that prevents an audio signal from exceeding a pre-determined level. Signals below this level are unaffected.

Low-Pass Filter

Circuit that passes signals below a set frequency and attenuates those above it.

mA

Abbreviation of *milliamp*, one-thousandth of an amp.

Memory

Circuit (for example, RAM) used to store digital data.

Microprocessor

Chip at the heart of desktop computers and other digital devices.

Modulate

To vary some aspect of a signal (or digital representation of a signal) by means of another signal or waveform.

Monitor

In recording terms, to monitor means to listen over loudspeakers or headphones. Studio loudspeakers and computer screens are also known as monitors.

Mono

Single channel of audio information to be reproduced over a single speaker. If multiple speakers are used, they all carry exactly the same signal.

Multitrack

Process of recording a piece of music using a multitrack recording device so that different parts may be recorded at different times.

Multitracker

Single piece of equipment that combines a multitrack tape recorder with a mixer.

Noise Gate

See *Gate*.

(Tape) Noise Reduction

Systems such as Dolby or dbx are specific examples of encode/decode noise-reduction systems, insomuch as they process the signal during recording and then apply the opposite process on playback. The processing is designed to bring about a decrease in tape hiss, although it doesn't affect any hiss recorded as part of the original signal.

Normalise

Socket wired so that the original signal path is unaffected unless a plug is inserted into the socket. Mixer insert points are normalised, as are some types of patchbay connection.

Octave

Range of frequencies where the upper limit is twice the lower frequency.

Offline

Describes a process that takes place in non-real time.

Ohm

Unit of electrical resistance.

Ohm's Law

Formula relating resistance, voltage and current in a resistive circuit. The formula is expressed as $I = V/R$, where I is the current in amps, V is the voltage and R is resistance in ohms.

Open Circuit

Break in a circuit preventing current flow.

Home Recording

Operating System

Basic housekeeping software used by a computer to allow it to run other software, communicate with peripherals and run a display.

Oscillator

Electronic circuit that produces a repeating waveform.

Overdub

To record onto a new track of a multitrack recorder while monitoring what has already been recorded on other tracks.

Overload

To exceed the limits for which a circuit has been designed.

Pad

Resistive circuit designed to reduce the level of a signal.

Pan Control

Control for moving a signal between left and right stereo extremes.

Parallel

Describes the connection of two or more electrical components or systems so that all their inputs are connected together and all their outputs are connected together.

Passive

Describes an electrical circuit that contains no active (amplifying) components. For example, a resistive pad is a passive circuit.

Parametric EQ

Band-pass equaliser providing independent control over cut/boost, frequency and bandwidth.

Patchbay

Array of panel-mounted connectors used to bring commonly used inputs and outputs to a central location. Signal routing is effected by using plug-in patch cords.

Patch Cord

Short cable designed to be used with a patchbay.

Phantom Power

System for supplying 48V power to balanced capacitor and electret mics via a standard mic cable. The phantom power source may be a stand-alone unit but is more often built into the mixing console or the mic preamp being used.

Phase

Timing difference between two identical sine waves, expressed in degrees, where 360° represents a delay of one complete cycle. A phase difference of 180° produces an inverted waveform, which, if added to the original, would cancel it out, resulting in no signal being produced.

Phaser

Modulated delay effect which mixes a signal with a phase-shifted version of itself to produce a filtering effect.

Phono Plug

Type of signal connector used on hi-fi and semi-pro recording equipment.

Pitch

Frequency of a musical note.

Power Supply

Converts mains electricity to the voltages required to power a piece of electronic equipment.

Post-Fade

Describes an aux signal derived after a mixer's channel fader so that the aux-send level reflects any channel-fader adjustments. Post-fade sends are generally used for feeding effects devices and may be referred to as *effect sends*.

Pre-Fade

Describes an aux signal derived from before the channel fader so that the aux-send level is independent of the channel-fader position. Pre-fade sends are often used for creating foldback (cue) mixes and may be referred to as *foldback controls*.

Punching In

Also known as *dropping in*, this describes the action of putting a tape track into Record mode while the tape is in motion in order to replace a specific section of a recording.

Punching Out

Action of terminating a punch-in by switching the tape machine out of Record mode.

Q

Measure of a filter circuit's resonance, defined as the centre frequency divided by the bandwidth.

RAM

Abbreviation of *random-access memory*, used by modern computer systems for the temporary storage of data.

R-DAT

Abbreviation of *rotary-head digital-audio tape (machine)*.

Real Time

Describes a process that takes place with no perceptible delay.

Resistance

Opposition to the flow of electric current, measured in ohms.

Resonance

Degree to which a filter circuit or mechanical resonator emphasises a particular frequency. (See *Q*.)

Reverberation

Natural effect created when a sound bounces off nearby solid surfaces in an enclosed space to the extent that the reflected sound can still be heard for a time after the original sound has ceased.

S/PDIF

Digital standard interfacing system for transferring stereo audio data from one piece of equipment to another via an RCA phono connector or optical cable.

Sampling

Process of digitising a signal by measuring successive points along an analogue waveform.

Home Recording

Separation

Ensuring that certain sounds are kept separate. In a studio where several musicians are playing together, each player's mic will tend to pick up some sound from the other instruments in the room. The lower the level of this unwanted spill, the better the separation.

Sequencer

Device for the recording, editing and playback of MIDI music compositions. May be computer-based or a piece of stand-alone hardware.

Signal

Any meaningful electrical information passing through an electronic system.

Signal-To-Noise Ratio

Ratio of the maximum signal level to the circuit noise or tape noise in decibels.

Short Circuit

Accidental signal path in a circuit between two points that are not normally connected.

Spill

Term used to describe unwanted sound leakage into microphones – for example, in a live situation, the drums and guitar amps will invariably spill into the vocal microphones.

SPL

Abbreviation of *sound-pressure level*.

Stereo

Describes a two-channel system feeding left and right loudspeakers in an attempt to recreate the way we perceive sounds coming from different directions.

Synthesiser

Musical instrument able to generate a wide variety of musically pitched sounds by electronic means.

Tracks

Originally a term referring to tape-based recording, *tracks* relates to the physical sections of tape used to store individual parts of a recording. Tracks are parallel to each other and are recorded and played back using a multisection head so as to keep them separate until they are mixed. The term *track* has now been carried over into the realm of digital tape and hard-disk recording systems, although it is mainly conceptual in this context insomuch as the data is not recorded on individual, parallel tracks.

Transpose

To change the key or pitch of a note or sequence of notes.

Tweeter

Speaker designed to handle only high frequencies.

Unbalanced

Describes a conventional audio connection with a single signal conductor surrounded by a screen.

Valve

Better known as a *tube* in the US, a valve is an active

circuit device comprising a heated cathode, a grid and an anode sealed in an evacuated glass or metal tube.

Vibrato

Musical, low-frequency modulation of pitch.

Volt

SI unit of electrical potential energy.

Watt

SI unit of electrical power.

Waveform

Visual representation of an electrical signal.

White Noise

Random electrical signal with equal average energy per Hertz.

Woofer

Loudspeaker designed to handle low frequencies.

XLR

Type of three-pin pro-audio connector often used to carry balanced audio signals, including those from microphones.

MIXER JARGON

Those Numbers!

If you see a mixer described as 24:8:24:2, the first number is the number of input channels. The second number (in this case, 8) means that the mixer has eight output groups. The third number tells us how many monitor channels the desk has, and if it's an in-line desk, this will be the same as the number of input channels. If, on the other hand, it is a split console, the number of monitor channels may well be less than the number of input channels. Finally, the number 2 indicates that the main output of the desk is stereo.

In-line

Describes a desk on which the monitor channel controls are located in the same-numbered strips as the input channels.

Split

Describes a desk on which the monitor channels are physically separate from the input channels and probably located in the master section, to the right of the console.

Mute

Most studio mixers have Mute buttons on their input channels that turn off both the channel signal and any post-fade aux (effects) sends. Pre-fade (foldback) sends are not normally affected.

PFL And Solo

PFL (Pre-Fade Listen) is a system that allows any selected channel or aux send/return to be heard in isolation over the studio monitors. Because PFL is pre-fade (ie monitored prior to the channel fader), the level is independent of the channel fader position. When a channel's PFL button is pressed, all the other channels (on which the PFL has not been pressed) are excluded from the monitor mix, and at the same time the signal

Home Recording

level of the channel currently being checked is displayed on one of the console's meters. PFL is generally used in this way to set up the input-gain trims of individual channels.

Solo

Isolates the channel in the monitor mix. Unlike PFL, however, the signal is post-fader, which means that what you hear is the actual level of the signal in the mix. Most solo systems also retain the pan position of the signal being checked, which is why the term SIP (Solo In Place) is also commonly used. On a studio console, the main stereo output feeding the master stereo recorder is not interrupted when PFL, Solo or SIP are used.

Aux Sends

Mixers invariably incorporate both pre-fade and post-fade aux sends. Aux sends provide a means of setting up an independent mix of the channel signals, either for feeding effects or for providing a foldback mix. Pre-fade sends aren't affected by changes in the channel-fader position, which makes them ideal for setting up foldback mixes. Post-fade sends are derived after the channel fader, so if the channel fader is adjusted, the aux-send level changes accordingly. This is necessary when adding effects such as echo or reverb because it's normally desirable for the relative levels of the dry signal and the effect to remain constant.

Insert Point

An insert point is simply a socket at which the signal flow may be interrupted, allowing an external signal processor to be connected – for example, a compressor or gate. Most consoles use TSR (Tip/Sleeve/Ring) stereo jacks as insert points, which means that a Y-lead (comprising a stereo jack at one end and two mono jacks at the other) is needed to connect the external device. Alternatively, the insert points may be wired to a normalised patchbay. Insert points are usually provided in the input channels, in the groups and at the main L/R stereo outputs.

Aux Return

An aux return is, in effect, an additional line-input channel but one with fewer facilities than the main input channels. On smaller desks, they will be permanently routed to the stereo mix buss, while larger desks will provide the same routing arrangement as the main input channels. Although aux sends are included for use with effects, they can be used to add any line-level signal (such as a tape machine, CD player or MIDI instrument) to the mix.

Monitor Outputs

Outputs designed to feed a pair of monitor speakers so that they can each be adjusted in level without actually affecting the signal being sent to the main mixer outputs. The monitor outputs can also be switched to monitor the solo buss, aux sends, aux returns and so on.